Lakota Culture, World Economy

Lakota Culture, World Economy

Kathleen Ann Pickering

UNIVERSITY OF NEBRASKA PRESS
LINCOLN AND LONDON

© 2000 by the University of Nebraska Press
Manufactured in the United States of America

Library of Congress Cataloging-in-Publication Data
Pickering, Kathleen Ann, 1958–
Lakota culture, world economy / Kathleen Ann Pickering.
p.   cm.
Includes bibliographical references and index.
ISBN 0-8032-3690-5 (cl.: alk. paper)
1. Teton Indians — Economic conditions.   2. Pine Ridge
Indian Reservation (S.D.) — Economic conditions.
3. Rosebud Indian Reservation (S.D.) — Economic conditions.
4. Teton Indians — Ethnic identity.   I. Title.
E99.T34 P53   2000
330.9783'6 — dc21   00-023482

To my parents, champions of their local community
and citizens of the world

Contents

Illustrations

Maps

Photographs

Preface

I approach a small home made from layers of wood planks and mortar. The back is surrounded by tall weeds, the front is encompassed in mud. Black plastic garbage bags and duct tape cover one corner of the roof. A sixty-year-old man greets me, his face worn and wrinkled from hard living. "We had some bad winds come through here a few weeks back and just took part of the roof right off." As we enter, a group of young children are told to go outside and play. The house is divided into two tiny bedrooms and one larger common area for three adults and five children. It is sparsely furnished with a hodgepodge of well-worn chairs. Nothing looks new. We sit on the portion of the sofa that still has seat cushions, and the man offers me coffee. In Lakota language, he directs his nephew, in his early thirties with long straight black hair in a ponytail, to make coffee. The white enamel stove is missing all its knobs and needs a match to light the burner. As we work through my questionnaire, the man recounts his work history. "I've tried hard to get something steady, but I only got CETA [Comprehensive Employment and Training Act] jobs, nothing permanent. I had a security job at the hospital, that was civil service, but then they changed it to a tribal contract and I was out. Then I was a janitor for five and a half years, but since 1984 it's been off and on. I was a janitor in Minneapolis for three months. Now I get SSI [Supplemental Security Income]." He lights a cigarette. "We make beadwork to sell. Before my wife passed away, we'd make doughnuts and sweet rolls to sell. She was a good cook. I buy meat and dry it, like jerky, and we sell Indian food sometimes. If I had a trailer, then I could sell more, a food trailer, but they cost $1,700 and it's hard to live on my income as it is."

On a worn linoleum and metal table sits a 1970s vintage color television hooked up to cable and playing throughout our conversation. We get to the portion of the questionnaire that deals with potential sources of credit, and I ask if he has ever pawned anything. "No, I never did. I don't got nothing to pawn. Except my poor TV, and I couldn't part with that." On the TV screen, Captain Kirk is instructing his men to prepare for the exploration of a new world.

The Lakotas of the Pine Ridge and Rosebud Reservations in rural South Dakota are poor. For more than a century, they have been relegated to the margins of the U.S. economy. Like many indigenous communities on the periphery of the world economy, the Lakotas confront such challenges as high unemployment, pressure to migrate for wage work, limited access to credit, and high rates of alcoholism. Yet the Lakotas continue to be distinct. Even in the late twentieth century, their language, styles of dress, religious practices, family organization, art, music, and social values coalesce into a collective sense of cultural identity for these reservation communities.

Culture and the world economy are inextricably woven into the Lakotas' lives. Each day, the Lakotas think and do things that make them distinctively Lakota, yet every day they also experience the far-flung effects of a global economic system. This book examines the connection between their indigenous culture and the world economy.

Focusing on the structures, processes, and events of everyday life that link the Pine Ridge and Rosebud Reservations to the world economic system, I address two questions in particular. First, how is the indigenous culture of the Lakotas maintained despite their continual economic incorporation? Through the fulcrum of the household, Lakotas confront manifestations of the world economy with distinctly cultural responses to production and consumption. Lakota households make decisions about what economic activities to engage in, within a limited palette of economic options. Lakota households also make decisions about what and how much to consume, within a boundless palette of goods and services offered at a price. These decisions and their transformation into practice reflect the imposition of indigenous cultural concerns onto the global economic system.

Second, given their cultural resistance, how are the Lakotas continually drawn into the world economy? The reasons for and mechanics of economic control are more easily understandable in situations in which core economic interests are intensively appropriating resources or labor from a peripheral region. How, then, do we explain economic control of places such as Pine Ridge and Rosebud, which attract far less attention by core economic interests? I identify two chief mechanisms of economic incorporation and control. First, aspects of Lakota social identity are manipulated to regulate economic opportunities and direct the flow of accumulated capital toward the beneficiaries of the world economy. Second, outside interests continually make efforts to define what the Lakota poor "need"; core interests continue to be the real beneficiaries of reservation programs for self-determination, economic development, or public assistance.

Lakota culture, particularly its social and religious aspects, is quite well known (see Bucko 1998; DeMallie 1978; DeMallie and Parks 1987; Grobsmith 1981; Hassrick 1964; Lewis 1990; Walker 1982; Young Bear and Theisz 1994). This culture is not independent of the forces of the world economy. As I argue, Lakota culture provides a counterpoint to external demands from the world economy. This dynamic tension between an indigenous local culture and the world economy helps shape contemporary Lakota culture and affects in varying degrees the trajectory of the global economic system.

I approach Lakota culture and the world economy in six chapters. In chapter 1, I briefly provide an overview of the history and economic composition of the Pine Ridge and Rosebud Reservations. In chapters 2, 3, and 4, I examine how production and consumption are interconnected on the reservations, highlighting the role of Lakota households in the dialectical process between local culture and the world economy. In chapters 5 and 6, I look at various mechanisms that help the world economy maintain control over the returns from economic activities at Pine Ridge and Rosebud.

More than ten years of work and research with the Lakota communities of Pine Ridge and Rosebud are invested in this book. From 1987 to 1989 I worked as managing attorney for the Pine Ridge branch office of Dakota Plains Legal Services, headquartered on the Rosebud Reservation. There I was exposed to the economic activities and difficulties facing Lakota households. In my search for answers about the extreme poverty on Pine Ridge and Rosebud, I eventually decided to return to graduate school. I conducted fieldwork on the Pine Ridge and Rosebud Indian Reservations from June through August 1991 and from June 1992 to July 1993. Each time I stayed with two families, one on each reservation. I have kept in contact with the people I have come to know well over the years, making regular visits to Pine Ridge and Rosebud for both social and academic reasons.

To reflect the tremendous diversity of opinion and experience among the Lakotas, I conducted one hundred detailed interviews in ten different communities within the Rosebud and Pine Ridge Reservations. They were the Pine Ridge Reservation villages of Pine Ridge Village, Kyle, Wanbli/Potato Creek, Wounded Knee/Manderson, Oglala, and Porcupine; and the Rosebud Reservation villages of Rosebud Village, St.

Francis, Antelope/Mission, and Parmelee (see map 2). Interviews were conducted informally in English, but a set of standard questions was covered in every interview. Participants were selected to represent a range of life experiences and economic opportunities corresponding with the 1980 U.S. Census figures for Standard Occupational Classification (see appendixes 1 and 2).

I also interviewed another 140 participants from Rosebud and Pine Ridge, some in less detail, others in depth about a single topic or concern. Ten additional interviews were conducted with Lakota people engaged in wage work in Denver, Rapid City, and Sioux Falls. The responses of these 150 participants are limited to anecdotal comments and are not reflected in the statistical figures presented here. I also attended public meetings, powwows, and social gatherings; followed the local media; and engaged in innumerable casual conversations.

Between February and October 1999, I conducted interviews with 25 households on Pine Ridge and Rosebud about changes related to welfare reform, and with 134 households on Pine Ridge about small business and microenterprise credit needs. Thirty-seven of these interviews were with households that participated in my initial study between 1991 and 1993.

In writing this book, I view my role in part as facilitator for the many voices of residents on the Pine Ridge and Rosebud Reservations. There are many, many voices and many perspectives. I did not select a list of criteria by which I determined an individual's beliefs or practices to be "authentic Lakota" and then ignore commentary that strayed from that criteria. I try not to privilege any one view but rather aim to capture a slice of the tremendous complexity, variability, and individuality that makes these reservations vibrant, enticing, and diverse, despite the superficial impressions created by a long history of poverty, oppression, and discrimination.

The Lakotas who contributed to this study were deeply concerned that they would be personally identified. Some were even hesitant to sign the human subjects informed consent form that ensured that their anonymity would be maintained. This anxiety over individual identification has its origins in many factors common to reservation life that may elude a visitor. An opinion or criticism of the contemporary political system or the current tribal administration may endanger the job security of relatives working as tribal or Bureau of Indian Affairs (BIA) employees. The revelation that an individual retains hidden assets may result in an attempted burglary or create resentments in the community over the failure to share that bounty. Information about income generated by economic activities may be used by social service offices, the BIA, or the state of

South Dakota to reduce or terminate forms of public assistance that are critical to Lakota household survival. Because of such complex economic, social, and political relationships and ramifications, I do not identify any individual directly or indirectly, having changed the location, type of occupation, or family composition to obscure individual identities.

The Lakota words used throughout this book have been systematically transcribed to conform to the DeMallie-Parks system of orthography.

I am indebted to a great number of people from Pine Ridge and Rosebud for their assistance and support, many of whom have asked not to be named. I am grateful to Lonnie Two Bear and her family for their limitless hospitality, generosity, and friendship. Viola Burnette has been a colleague, mentor, and friend for me, and *učí* (grandmother) for my children. Elsie Meeks and the staff of the Lakota Fund have provided unending support and assistance. I am especially grateful to the many Lakota families I approached only once for an interview and who gave graciously and generously of their time, experience, and insights.

To supplement information gathered from interviews, I conducted archival research at the National Archives in Washington DC, the Federal Archives Research Center in Kansas City, the South Dakota Historical Society in Pierre, the Doris Duke Oral History Project at the University of South Dakota in Vermillion, and the Jesuit Archives at Marquette University in Milwaukee. I want especially to thank Alan Perry at the Federal Archives Research Center and LaVera Rose at the South Dakota Historical Society for their help.

I am grateful to the members of my defense committee at the University of Wisconsin-Madison — Katherine Bowie, Gary Feinman, Peter Nabokov, Matt Snipp, and Neil Whitehead — for their help in transforming my dissertation into this book. I also thank Thomas D. Hall and the anonymous reviewers for the University of Nebraska Press for their illuminating, detailed, and valuable comments. Finally, I thank my husband, David Mushinski, for his economic analysis, for his moral support, and most of all for his help in transforming our lives from corporate lawyers in Boston to social scientists in Pine Ridge and Rosebud.

The research and writing of this book was funded by several sources: a National Science Foundation Fellowship; National Science Foundation Dissertation Improvement Grant no. SBR-9221383; Wenner-Gren Predoctoral Small Grant no. 5473; a Colorado State University Faculty Research Grant and Career Enhancement Grant; and USDA Cooperative Agreement no. 43-3-AEN-7-80065, Gene Summers, principal investigator, and the Wisconsin Agricultural Experiment Station.

Lakota Culture, World Economy

Map 1. The Pine Ridge and Rosebud Reservations and surrounding area

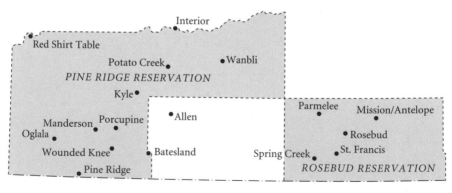

Map 2. Communities of the Pine Ridge and Rosebud Reservations

1
A History and Overview
of the Lakota Economy

Looking at both the Pine Ridge and Rosebud Reservations is like get-ting to know two sisters. To outsiders, the similarities between the reser-vations are remarkable. To those living on the reservations, however, it is the differences between Pine Ridge and Rosebud that tend to domi-nate conversation. When Lakotas are asked about their economic atti-tudes and experiences in general, the responses of men and women from the Pine Ridge and the Rosebud Reservations highly correspond. When asked to compare their experiences and attitudes with those of their sister reservation, however, Lakotas frequently emphasize differences, as if the two reservations were worlds apart. A similar relationship exists among Lakotas from different villages within the same reservation. For example, when asked about the economic conditions on the reservation as a whole, people from Pine Ridge Village and from Wanbli have similar concerns and observations. But these same men and women highlight distinctive characteristics when asked to compare the two communities specifically.

The social and economic connections between the two reservations are strong. Many Lakotas have land, relatives, and personal histories that span both, and marriage between enrolled members of Pine Ridge and Rosebud is extremely common. Job opportunities often determine which reservation a family ultimately chooses to live on.

Each reservation harbors special perceptions of the other that are shared in jokes and stories. People in Rosebud often mention being afraid of Pine Ridgers, finding them more violent, radical, and aggressive. The perception in Rosebud is that Rosebud's men are more "gainfully em-ployed" than those in Pine Ridge and that Pine Ridge's women are more "gainfully employed" than Pine Ridge's men. Pine Ridge residents often note that Lakotas in Rosebud have given up more of their traditional practices to accommodate non-Indians and their economic interests. People in Rosebud feel that Pine Ridge is more culturally intact, with more native-language speakers and more households adhering to Lakota traditions in their daily lives. At the same time, people in Pine Ridge think the Lakotas at Rosebud are "more into Indians," understanding the value of working to preserve cultural traditions.

Although I acknowledge such differences in perceptions, I emphasize here the commonalities of the attitudes and experiences that bind Pine Ridge and Rosebud into a coherent economic arena. The residents of these two reservations participate in the same slice of a larger economic system and employ similar cultural mechanisms to deal with that system.

Prereservation History

The residents of Pine Ridge and Rosebud are part of the Lakota-speaking group of the Siouan language family, also known as the Teton Sioux. The Oglalas, Sicangus, Hunkpapas, Minneconjous, Sans Arcs, Two Kettles, and Blackfeet are each subdivisions of the Lakota or Teton Sioux (Walker 1982:19). Originally living in the region that became the state of Minnesota, the Lakota people experienced dramatic changes in their culture and society between 1650 and 1880 as they migrated to the Plains and developed an economic strategy centered on the buffalo and the horse (Bamforth 1988:91; Hyde 1937:3, 9, 11; Hyde 1961:3–4; Neill 1881:9, 42; Thwaites 1895:23:225).

Social Organization

Before the establishment of Pine Ridge and Rosebud, Lakota social organization was tremendously fluid (Henning 1982:58; Price 1996:6–7; see Myers 1988:269). The smallest unit was the single-family household. A group of households, consisting of relatives by blood, marriage, or social convention, formed the *tiyóšpaye* (extended family unit), the most basic unit of Lakota social organization. In aggregation, a number of *tiyóšpaye* made up one of the seven distinct Lakota subdivisions, such as the Oglalas or the Sicangus (E. Deloria 1944:40–41; Holder 1970:102; Hyde 1937: 309; Walker 1982:3–4). Each member of the *tiyóšpaye* had mutual obligations of support and generosity (E. Deloria 1944:40–41; DeMallie 1979: 233; Schusky 1986:68). At any given time, an individual or household unhappy with interpersonal relations or material opportunities within a *tiyóšpaye* could split off and either form a new group or join another existing group (Howard 1960:264; T. Kehoe 1983:329; Walker 1982:24). Consequently, a group such as the Oglalas often included members from other subdivisions, such as the Sicangus or Hunkpapas. Intermarriage between subdivisions was also frequent (Hyde 1937:31; Medicine 1983a: 273; Smith 1970:89; Thwaites 1902:38–39; Walker 1982:7, 16).

Related households or *tiyóšpaye* lived together throughout most of the year, and each had a nominal leader, although the method of decision making was group consensus (Neill 1881:44; Price 1996:7–8; Schusky 1986:68–69). There are suggestions that heredity played a role in determining the position of leader within a *tiyóšpaye*, but, in fact, leadership was often based on superior abilities, authority, and influence with the people (Holder 1970:102; Hyde 1937:30, 308; Walker 1982:24).

Each Lakota subdivision had an all-male council that consisted of the leaders of various *tiyóšpaye:* spiritual leaders, elders, accomplished hunters, and other men excelling in camp selection or other critical activities. This council made decisions about when and where to relocate or conduct communal hunts and about other matters of concern to the subdivision as a whole. The council members gained no particular distinction or material advantage from their position, but they received respect, generosity, and most critically social, political, and economic support in return for their ability and insight (Holder 1970:102; Hyde 1937:309; Kelly 1962:87; Pond 1986:68; Price 1996:9–11; Walker 1982:22–23, 126–27). No formal overarching political structure, such as a state or national government, existed for the Lakotas as a whole (Dorsey 1897:221; Goldfrank 1943:69; Hickson 1974:23; Kroeber 1939:149; see Hindess and Hirst 1975: 41). But even though each subdivision was politically autonomous and thus potentially in conflict with the others, religious traditions helped mitigate any hostility that emerged. White Buffalo Calf Woman had appeared to the Lakotas with a sacred pipe that they were instructed to smoke, thereby committing themselves to certain spiritual practices that depended on intratribal peace and cooperation (Mallery 1893:290–91; Melody 1980:4–5, 9; Mooney 1896:1062; Price 1996:2; Smith 1970:87–88; Steinmetz 1980:17).

Economic History

The economic and political incorporation of the Lakotas into the world economy was well under way by 1725 (Hanson 1975:4; Henning 1982:59; Holder 1970:79, 99; Hyde 1937:8–9; Reher & Frison 1980:34; White 1978: 323; Wissler 1914:5; Wolf 1982:177). Like most American Indian societies, Lakotas experienced two dramatic periods of incorporation, the fur trade and the formation of reservations.

For generations before their confinement to reservations, Lakotas directly and indirectly traded fur and meat products for plant resources and manufactured items. Wider indigenous networks of trade connected the Lakotas with Upper Missouri River horticulturists and with groups from New Mexico to the southwest, the Hudson Bay to the north, and the

Rockies and Pacific coast to the west (Blakeslee 1977:80; Blakeslee 1981: 94; Kenner 1969:7–8, 11; Wood & Thiessen 1985:48; Wood 1980:99–100). Horses, guns, and other Euro-American manufactured items were incorporated into these preexisting intertribal networks (Ewers 1968:22; Schilz & Worcester 1987:7–8; Wissler 1914:10–11; Wood 1980:100). Horses came to symbolize wealth and were a favored gift and exchange item (Hanson 1975:101; Hyde 1937:30; Roe 1955:20–21, 62, 68, 190, 267; Wissler 1938: 161). The Lakotas aggressively eliminated tribes competing for the same trade and used intimidation to create incentives for trade with hesitant or unwilling tribes (Will and Hyde 1917:184–87).

By the early 1800s, the European fur market had shifted from the nearly extinct American beaver to buffalo hides. Large numbers of traders and explorers traveling through the Plains also increased demand for dried buffalo meat provisions (Wolf 1982:176). The growing economic importance of the buffalo coincided with an increase in the hunting capacity of the Lakotas, owing to the acquisition of horses and metal implements (Klein 1983:146–47; Roe 1955:93, 177–78). Euro-American traders and government officials delivered vast amounts of trade goods, weapons, and treaty annuities to particular Lakota men who, some charge, agreed to pursue outside objectives often at the expense of their own. These men in turn gained power by controlling the distribution of these goods, regardless of their status within the *tiyóšpaye* (One Feather 1974; Schusky 1986:71–72). By the end of the nineteenth century, the Lakotas had developed a political system that was compatible with regional, U.S., and international demands for representative decision making and elite rule (Schusky 1986:81; see Wallerstein 1991).

As Lakota reliance on trade goods increased in the nineteenth century, buffalo herds decreased (Denig 1961:25; Mooney 1896:825). The systematic and highly organized exploitation of buffalo for the fur and meat trade outstripped animal reproduction (Holder 1970:114, 123; Roe 1955: 182, 190–92). At the same time, the interests of the world economy in the U.S. Plains shifted from furs to agriculture. By 1870, because of a decline in the global demand for furs, the number of trading facilities in Lakota territory decreased significantly (Pickering 1994:62–63).

As U.S. military pressure mounted and settler interests in land and agricultural production intensified, the Lakotas ceded land in a series of agreements, including the Fort Laramie Treaty of 1868. In exchange for land cessions, the treaties provided rations, annuity goods, and other forms of economic and social support, as well as an explicit acknowledgment of the Lakotas' status as a sovereign tribal entity (Hurt 1987:65, 85; Hyde 1937:40, 51, 56; Olson 1965:7–8, 27–39; Roe 1955:194; Utley 1984:

178–80; Viola 1974:7, 20). The decrease in land base exacerbated the insufficiency of buffalo and other animal resources to sustain Lakota communities (Hyde 1937:34–35, 56, 63, 280–81; Olson 1965:229; Roe 1955:192).

The Pine Ridge and Rosebud Agencies were established in 1878. With the partitioning of the Great Sioux Reservation by the Great Sioux Agreement in 1889, these agencies became the Pine Ridge and Rosebud Indian Reservations in south-central South Dakota on the Nebraska border.

The Current Reservation Setting

Pine Ridge Village is the employment center on the Pine Ridge Reservation. Clues where people work are revealed by the scattered buildings that make up this Bureau of Indian Affairs (BIA) Agency town. The overwhelming number of signs relate to federal and tribal office buildings: Indian Health Service Hospital, Indian Housing Authority, OST (Oglala Sioux Tribe) Sewer and Water, BIA Headquarters, OST Courthouse, Red Cloud Tribal Office Building, and Pine Ridge High School. A couple of convenience stores, gas stations, video stores, fast-food restaurants, and a grocery store are the full extent of the private sector. Dakota Plains Legal Services, Sue Ann Big Crow Youth Center, the Holy Rosary Mission, and a number of other churches comprise the local nonprofit organizations. Given a drive of at least thirty miles and as much as one hundred miles from the last "real" town, the first-time visitor is often left looking for more.

The village of Kyle, some forty-five miles northeast of Pine Ridge Village, plays a growing role in providing reservation employment opportunities. For the last five years, Kyle has attracted ongoing construction work and the prospect of new office jobs. Oglala Lakota College headquarters, OST Parks and Recreation offices, an Indian Health Services clinic, a tribal courthouse branch, the Mni Wiconi rural water project, the nonprofit Lakota Fund building, and a convenience store all occupy buildings recently constructed in the village. In contrast, smaller villages such as Red Shirt Table and Potato Creek offer virtually no wage labor opportunities (see map 2).

Rosebud Reservation is less centralized. The town of Mission houses the bulk of state and county offices, some federal government offices, and most commercial operations — the two largest reservation grocery stores, a hardware store, two motels, two video stores, and two gas stations with convenience stores — as well as the largest campus of Sinte Gleska University. Most of the tribal and federal government offices are located in Rosebud Village, along with Sinte Gleska University's main offices. The village of St. Francis boasts the headquarters of the St. Francis Jesuit Mission.

Social Organization and Values

Family is the primary social unit for interaction on the reservations. Several people mentioned to me that it was unusual to go visit or talk with someone outside their family. Some families continue to refer to themselves as *tiyóšpaye,* particularly in Pine Ridge (One Feather 1974). Most of the *tiyóšpaye* have been through numerous shifts in location and membership since reservation residence, as U.S. policies of land allotment, treaty annuity distributions, and relief projects created local political tensions (Biolsi 1992:104–5). Many elders feel that even families are not as close as they used to be, noting that in the past it had been common to go visit a relative on another part of the reservation. "People went visiting by wagon," an elder woman from Oglala remembers, "and when they got to your place, they'd stay overnight, maybe camp out even for two or three months at their relatives, and then go back to their own place. People don't do that anymore. The families aren't close like that, and people are always running around here and there."

Yet, of all the aspects identified as fundamental to Lakota culture, the importance of relatives and the obligations of each individual to his or her relatives is still the most pervasive. "When Wóȟpe, daughter of Maȟpíyatho, came before the people as White Buffalo Calf Woman, she brought two very important laws: Respect your elders and take care of your relatives. These laws were the basis for the *tiyóšpaye.* When wise men speak at feasts and meetings, they always remind the people that these laws are important to the Sioux people" (One Feather 1974:21). The phrase *Mitákuye Oyás'į,* translated "All my relatives," is used as the ending to prayers, speeches, and editorials. As one Rosebud spiritual leader explained: "*Mitákuye Oyás'į*" means you have to learn to be a relative to all living things and all things of the earth. The flowering of the Sacred Tree is our thoughts and the fruits are our feelings. *Thiwáhe,* the family, is one tree, male, female, and children. The way you know if it is a good strong tree is its relationship to other trees."

This conception of relatives influences the way household, family, and community social relations work on Pine Ridge and Rosebud. Lakotas use the terms grandmother, aunt, daughter, and grandchild to apply to a broad range of relationships, some consistent with Western kinship, some consistent with Lakota kinship, and some purely fictive. Lakota kinship addresses the mother and all her sisters as *iná* or mother, and all the children of her sisters as siblings. Similarly, the father and all his brothers are addressed as *até,* and all the children of his brothers as siblings. The Lakota terms for grandmother, grandfather, and grandchild are used more generally for those much older or much younger than the age of the speaker. In Lakota language, one is taught to address every person by his or her kinship term or, if no direct relationship exists, to call him or her the Lakota equivalent of cousin (White Hat 1999:15).

Generosity has been an enduring central social virtue in Lakota communities (Mekeel 1936:3; Mirsky 1937:388–89). It is common for people to fill the short-term needs of the entire extended family rather than to accumulate long-term assets for themselves or their nuclear families. To the extent savings are accumulated, they are used for community "giveaways" or public displays of generosity, not for direct future personal consumption. Despite the criticisms of Christian reformers, agents, and scholars that the redistribution of property kept any Lakota person from "getting ahead" (Mekeel 1936:11; Useem, Macgregor & Useem 1943:1), the importance of holding giveaways and sponsoring public meals for the community continues, even though the occasions for having such public gatherings have changed over time (E. Deloria 1944:77–78; Goldfrank 1943:79–81; A. Kehoe 1989:65). Honoring ceremonies, memorials for departed loved ones, and naming and adoption ceremonies are among the occasions for giveaways. The Lakota giveaway is an example of "reciprocal exchange" that "serves the function of cementing relationships, expressing mutual affection, and establishing a system of what the Lakota call 'Indian insurance'" (Grobsmith 1981:129–30).

Giveaways are often combined with powwows, Indian social dances divided by gender and styles of dance and accompanied by drumming and singing. Over the last fifty years, powwows have evolved into intertribal events that follow a standard progression and form, whether the host community is Lakota, Oneida, or an urban Indian center. Powwows take place year round, but the greatest number and most elaborate of events occur over the summer months in outdoor dance circles.

Housing

Housing is extremely limited on both reservations, because of the almost nonexistent private housing market. Furthermore, the main housing provider, the U.S. Department of Housing and Urban Development (HUD), faced annual budget cuts, misappropriations, and policy shifts through the 1980s, all of which had a negative impact on the reservation housing pool.

Two main residence patterns developed on the reservations. The first involves Lakotas who were and have remained on their individual land allotments. Their homesites often started with a log house, sometimes coupled with tents or tipis. Over time, these were replaced with trailer homes or frame houses self-constructed or built by HUD home-ownership and other housing programs, such as the BIA Housing Improvement Program (HIP). Several related families often live along the same country road or within the same large compound. During the early reservation period, family residence patterns continued to follow the *tiyóšpaye* grouping of related families living in one camp (Albers 1983: 184–86; Albers 1982:254; Carlson 1981:86, 105–6; Hurt 1987:139). When the BIA created reservation districts for representative tribal governments in the 1930s, members of the same *tiyóšpaye* were often clustered within a single district. As a consequence, many of the village and district names are related to the names of leaders of various *tiyóšpaye* at the time of reservation settlement. These settlements are often associated with the most "traditional" families, who moved as far away from the BIA agency and the appendage tribal government as possible to avoid white interference (V. Deloria & Lytle 1984:233; Wax, Wax & Dumont 1964:30).

The second housing pattern began in the 1960s when HUD built clusters of single-family homes in the model of tiny suburbs, designed to provide efficient access to water and electricity and thus help modernize isolated communities. Such clusters are scattered across the reservations, often near areas where *tiyóšpaye* were living, such as Red Shirt Table and He Dog. The clusters introduce a certain dissonance to the landscape. Thirty miles from any semblance of a town and surrounded by wide open spaces, one suddenly drives past a group of a dozen or more identical houses crammed together on tiny lots, arranged side by side in straight rows. Because of dissatisfaction with the conditions in cluster housing, many Lakotas are now moving back to the country, either to their allotments or to new homesites.

The waiting list for any HUD housing is considerable. In Pine Ridge, no new housing units were constructed during a ten-year period from the late 1970s until the late 1980s. One woman waited more than ten years before her family was assigned a HUD home-ownership unit. Because of the demand, preference is given to families with children, so there is virtually no chance for single people to own or rent their own housing. There is no right of sublease for HUD rental units, so families who must leave the reservation for short-term employment or educational opportunities lose their homes.

Federal housing programs have distorted the development of market-priced housing, creating contradictory incentives for reservation residents. The cost of both HUD rental housing and home-ownership units is determined by the amount of household income, as governed by HUD regulations and local policies set by the local Indian Housing Authority. Those with household income below a certain level receive what is termed "negative rent," meaning cash of up to $128 per month supplied by the Housing Authority to help pay public utility providers for electricity and heating costs. Conversely, those with several full-time wage workers in the household must pay 25 percent of their combined salaries as rent for the exact same housing unit for which their neighbor may receive negative rent. As one Rosebud wage worker notes: "It's really unfair, because there are no ceilings on the payments made on either low-income or home-ownership units, so if a family is making only AFDC [Aid to Families with Dependent Children], they will pay $65 a month, and if a family has two or three members with full-time jobs, they'll pay $800 a month for the same housing, or purchase the same house for either $15,000 or $100,000. Apparently, HUD has written to the Rosebud Housing Authority and indicated that they can set ceilings if they want to, but so far Housing has taken the position that the regulations prevent them from putting in payment ceilings." The same regulations work in urban areas; people who can afford higher rent move to higher-rent housing. With no private housing market to speak of on the reservations, people with wage-labor jobs have the same housing pool as people with little or no cash income. Passage of the Native American Housing Assistance and Self-Determination Act of 1996 separated Indian housing from public housing for the first time and removed Indian housing from HUD guidelines that had been developed with mostly urban Americans in mind, giving tribes the opportunity to create regulations that are better suited to the reservation setting (NAIHC 1996).

Other federally funded housing is available for teachers and hospital workers at their work site, but it is limited in size and restricted to immediate family. The rent for teacher housing is approximately $170 per month, deducted from the teacher's paycheck. Rosebud also has a series of elderly housing apartment units, and there is an elderly residential home in Pine Ridge.

In addition to HUD home ownerships, a handful of privately owned trailers, HIP houses, log homes, and a smattering of homes with private mortgages fill in the rest of the housing picture. Trailer homes, the most prevalent form of housing outside HUD programs, vary from spacious, modern, and new to the oldest models with no utilities and tiny rooms. Even though there are many veterans in the reservation population, Veterans Administration home loans have had a minimal showing on Pine Ridge and Rosebud. According to the 1990 census, 39 percent of the homes in Rosebud and 40 percent of the homes in Pine Ridge are owner-occupied housing.

Because housing is limited, space is at a premium in most homes. Living rooms often double as bedrooms, either on a permanent basis or for visiting friends and relatives. Few households have the luxury of a separate room for sewing, woodwork, beading, or other microenterprise activity, so household demands on the common living area limit the time available for microenterprise production. Close quarters make it difficult for young people to socialize in the home, but there are few formal alternatives.

Household Composition

Lakota households are flexibly composed of members whose characteristics affect the type and range of resources and opportunities available to the household from both the capitalist market and local cultural networks. The spectrum of household members ranges from an extremely stable nuclear family to an extremely fluctuating group of individuals defined as relatives only in the broadest sense of Lakota kinship. Fluidly made up of immediate and extended family members, Lakota households are continually reconfigured. The composition of a given household is the result of a mixture of individual choices, social rights and obligations, and external factors such as demographics, the location of employment, the availability of housing, and housing costs. Being part of a household economic unit both adds economic burdens to Lakotas and offers avenues for resources that might not otherwise be available. The fluid and diverse composition of a typical Lakota household helps its members maintain access to all forms of income-generating resources, including wages, household production, and government assistance. Perhaps more important, a household can provide support during slow wage times, when only part-time work is available or there are seasonal layoffs.

The housing market affects the composition of households. Limited housing availability puts upward pressure on the number of people living together. The 1990 census reported an average of 4.51 persons living in a Pine Ridge household and an average of 3.91 persons living in a Rosebud household. These figures seem low. The average number of household members for those participating in this study is 5.7. A worker for the Indian Housing Authority notes that in certain communities as many as seven families live in a home designed for one.

Extended family members are commonly accepted into a household as temporary residents. For those waiting or ineligible for HUD homes, relatives are the main source of alternative living arrangements. One couple rented the home owned by the wife's sister, who was currently living with her husband's family. Another woman lived with her son until a rental unit in the same housing cluster became available for her, her daughter, and several grandchildren.

The complexity of the economic structure of households and the mutual support they provide is intensified by the tremendous mobility of reservation residents (Snipp 1996:45). If we use social relations rather than physical locations to conceptualize the construction of society, we find that "the relatively stable communities and networks of kinship, of friendship, of work and of leisure" are "the warp . . . everywhere shot through with the woof of human motion, as more persons and groups deal with the realities of having to move, or the fantasies of wanting to move" (Appadurai 1990:297). Summers are times of high mobility, as many short-term visitors join households. "I can't sit and quill in the summer—we have visitors from other tribes and whites," one Lakota woman told me. Relatives come and go as work opportunities appear and vanish or as love relationships begin and end. Relatives returning from off-reservation work are another common component of households, for the short term or sometimes for the long term. One Porcupine woman recalls, "We lived with my aunt when we moved back to Pine Ridge."

Children

Within the reservation communities it does take a village to raise a child. The costs of children are not borne entirely by their parents, and in some instances are not at all. Several mechanisms spread economic responsibility for children across the community. According to Lakota beliefs, children are innocent and should be cared for with lenience. The general community is expected to support children, watching out for them, feeding them, and taking them home. Many people feel a strong responsibility toward the children of any close relative. As one Pine Ridge woman explains, "Our second daughter is really my husband's niece. She was living in Denver as a baby and her real father abused her and ended up going to prison for it, so my husband figured we could keep her here. Initially, it was a full-time job, but now she's so well adjusted, he feels like he really did his part for the family."

The presence of parents in a child's household can be fluid, owing partly to a high divorce rate and open relationships outside marriage. Some children with divorced parents have living arrangements with both parents, adding to the fluctuating composition of their households. The strong social support between adult brothers and sisters also makes it easier to provide a stable family surrounding for children, with short- or long-term care available during changing marital relationships.

As in the past, grandparents often raise their grandchildren as if they were the natural parents. Even after parents reach maturity, it is still common for children to be raised by or spend long periods of time with their grandparents. This is especially true when parents are engaged in off-reservation work. People on the whole look forward to having many grandchildren, as one Oglala woman points out: "I hardly have any grandkids at all, not even twenty." Many people mention that they developed respect for the elderly through their relationship with their grandparents. One Wanbli woman recalls: "My grandparents really raised me; they gave me the knowledge that I have. They know how to express their opinions. You'll see the fifteenth van load of elders heading for Pine Ridge whenever the Grey Eagles have an issue and they send out the word that they need to go to a session of the council."

Children born to unmarried teenage girls are frequent additions to households (Snipp 1996:27). Many different attitudes exist about birth out of wedlock. Some Lakotas feel that under-age parents should take responsibility for the child, whether they are married or not. One Kyle woman expresses her family's attitude toward her teenage daughter's baby: "My sisters say that if my daughter is going to stay with that guy, then they should keep the baby with them, because the baby should have its parents, rather than always leaving her off with other people." Others accept that the proper place for the child is with the grandparents.

Facilities and Logistics

After spending time on Pine Ridge and Rosebud Reservations, one develops the equivalent of a type of night vision for locations and activities. The first-time visitor sees a sparsity of places to go and things to do. The long-term Lakota resident views the same scene as a wealth of opportunities and events. Sales from homes of outstanding beaders, daycare centers, country music dances, bingo, high school basketball, and traditional religious ceremonies are all taking place, well publicized through the networks of personal communication but with minimal outside fanfare or formal advertisement. Distances that might feel interminable to visitors become weekly or even daily jaunts as residents gather for special occasions in various communities or travel for specific needs such as banking or shopping.

The main government offices are in sprawling buildings of concrete, brick, and tile resembling elementary schools and other public buildings of the 1960s, complete with long tiled hallways and offices with multiple rows of desks. A few offices are housed in two-story formidable-looking brick structures from the early reservation days, buildings reminiscent of officer housing at a nineteenth-century fort. Still other offices are crammed into double-wide trailers, old church buildings, prefabricated buildings with metal siding, and other miscellaneous structures. The government offices lag in technology. For every office with computer terminals, there are an equal or greater number where typewriters drown out conversation. Even in some of the most complicated sectors of Bureau of Indian Affairs administration, such as landownership and lease income distribution, records are still being updated manually in oversized leather-bound notebooks and stored in massive wooden file cabinets.

Economic Activities

The contemporary economies of the Pine Ridge and Rosebud Reservations center on four main areas of work. Lakota households engage in a combination of wage work, small business and agricultural enterprises, microenterprise, and household subsistence activities. Public assistance is another area of minimal and constantly changing financial supplementation. Although no single activity offers assurances of economic support, the combination of activities and the fluid composition of household members provide ongoing access to at least minimal economic resources.

The demographics of the reservation population has an impact on economic productivity. The number of people of working age represents a smaller portion of the overall population than in the average U.S. community. In 1990, 47.7 percent of the population in Pine Ridge and 43.9 percent of the population in Rosebud was younger than sixteen years of age. The draw of off-reservation wage opportunities and federal programs such as urban relocation, whose explicit goal was moving working-age men and women off the reservation, have left reservations with a disproportionate number of young children and elderly people, those who are least able to develop an economic base for a truly vibrant local economy or independent tribal government (Albers 1983:198, 201; Neils 1971:46–57, 91–104, 111–16). A lower median age also means lower income, higher unemployment, higher crime, a greater proportion of unwed mothers, and more dependence on welfare (Wilson 1987:142).

2
Culture in Market Production

Because of the peripheral position of the Pine Ridge and Rosebud Reservations within the U.S. economy, Lakotas have difficulty finding access to market-based forms of production. Wage work positions, small business ownership, and commodity agricultural enterprises are at a premium, and unemployment and underemployment rates are high.

The demands of the world economy are readily felt in the wage labor jobs that are available. With virtually no bargaining power, Lakota wage workers face difficult working conditions with limited opportunities for advancement and constant pressures to leave their reservation communities to find better economic options. Lakota culture plays a crucial role in the way the workplace is experienced and tolerated. The ability to leave negative wage work conditions or survive unpredictable layoffs or termination turns in large part on the cultural values and local social networks that form a safety net for Lakota communities.

The tensions felt between local Lakota concerns and the demands of the world economy are most evident for those working in Lakota nonprofit organizations. Communities expect nonprofit organizations to provide services that reflect Lakota cultural values. Requirements imposed by the federal government on entities seeking charitable contributions, however, often interfere with the ability of nonprofit organizations to employ Lakota approaches for the good of Lakota people.

Lakota small businesses are few and far between. The world economy encourages Lakota enterprises to mirror the characteristics of other businesses in mainstream society to be competitive. At the same time, the local community expects Lakota businesses to behave in a manner that distinguishes them from the mainstream businesses well known for mistreating and exploiting Lakota customers. Integrating Lakota values into business operations has created special pressures as well as unique responses from Lakota entrepreneurs who have undertaken the challenge.

The Universe of Wage Work

The unemployment figures for both Rosebud and Pine Ridge are consistently high. Independent calculations of unemployment are made by the U.S. Census Bureau and the Bureau of Indian Affairs. The U.S. Census and Bureau of Labor Statistics calculate the percentage of working-age individuals who are "actively looking for work" but have not found work; these people are considered unemployed. Individuals who have realistically despaired of finding jobs are not considered "in the labor force," however. In the 1980 U.S. census, the unemployment rate for Rosebud Reservation's American Indian population of 5,643 was 35 percent, slightly lower than the 38 percent unemployment for Pine Ridge Reservation's American Indian population of 11,867. In 1990, the U.S. census reported 29.5 percent unemployment for the 7,998 native people at Rosebud and 32.7 percent for Pine Ridge's American Indian population of 11,006. The 1990 figures have been particularly criticized for their low population estimates for Pine Ridge and Rosebud and the inadequate funding provided to census takers for transportation to remote villages on the reservations. A full 53 percent of the working-age population in Pine Ridge was not "in the labor force" in 1990. Even the South Dakota Department of Labor noted in its *Labor Availability Study* for the Pine Ridge Reservation that of those not in the labor force, "many of these people would be willing to accept a job if one became available" (South Dakota Department of Labor 1991).

The BIA, however, does not exclude individuals from the labor force for not actively looking for work if they are otherwise able-bodied, not students, and not primary child-care providers. The BIA figures also benefit from more accurate information about the actual population size and economic status of reservation residents. The BIA unemployment figure for Pine Ridge in 1989 was 73 percent; for Rosebud, it was 86 percent (South Dakota Department of Labor 1991; BIA Statistics 1989; Hargreaves & Chang 1989:6).

The unemployment figures from both sources suggest that, for the most part, people in Pine Ridge and Rosebud have not participated in wage labor. The statistics, however, are somewhat misleading. Despite the BIA's calculation of an 86 percent unemployment rate in Rosebud during my period of research, more than 90 percent of those I spoke with had at least some wage work experience during their lifetime. Among those interviewed, 43 percent were currently without wage work, but 86 percent of those currently unemployed had had previous wage work experience.

In addition to high unemployment, underemployment is severe: many individuals find only seasonal jobs for a few weeks a year. In the 1990 U.S. census, of the individuals who were employed, 37 percent of those in Pine Ridge and 32 percent of those in Rosebud were employed for less than fourteen weeks during the year, and 57 percent of those in Pine Ridge and 54 percent of those in Rosebud were employed for less than half the year. Underemployment has been a long-term condition on the reservations. For example, in 1943, the average job span for Lakota men, from a sample of 225 adults, was 3.5 months (Useem, Macgregor & Useem 1943:2).

The largest single employer on both reservations is the federal government, followed by the respective tribal governments. In Pine Ridge, not only did government jobs account for the greatest portion of nonfarm wage and salary employment in 1990, representing 35 percent of the jobs by industry, but they also provided the highest average weekly earnings, $409.49 (South Dakota Department of Labor 1991). According to the 1990 U.S. census, federal government positions accounted for 25 percent of all jobs in Pine Ridge and 28 percent in Rosebud. Local government accounted for another 33 percent of the jobs in Pine Ridge and 14 percent of the jobs in Rosebud.

Federal government workers tend to have the longest terms of employment with one employer, although their specific jobs frequently change over the years. For example, an Antelope man held several positions during the twenty years he worked for the BIA: "I was a dorm night attendant, an instructional aide, and the last 12 years I worked in adult vocational training, until I retired in 1985." Before Congress included Indian preference in hiring in the enabling legislation of federal Indian agencies in the 1970s, the government positions filled by Lakota workers tended to be exclusively manual and support positions (Stubben 1994: 111). In the 1940s, local wage work was often available in road and building construction or in freighting items from the railroad, mostly on a temporary basis (E. Deloria 1944:94–95; Macgregor 1946:46). Beginning in the late 1970s, Lakota people filled the bulk of managerial, supervisory, and directors' positions in the various BIA offices and programs.

Within the tribal government, there are a small number of elected positions and a larger pool of nonelected jobs. Another set of positions are nonelected but require approval by the tribal council. They include the chief judge and associate judges of the tribal court, chief of police, and positions in other tribal programs that have been contracted from the federal government. The elected positions are tribal president, vice president, and councilmen for each of the reservation districts, based on population.

The largest group of tribal positions are nonelected and bureaucratic.

These include directors and administrators of the various tribal programs, such as elderly nutrition, the Tribal Land Enterprise, the Tribal Employment Rights Office (TERO, called Tribal Employment Contracts and Rights Office [TECRO] in Rosebud), Tribal Parks and Recreation, the office of tribal taxation and business licenses, and a tribally operated alcohol treatment center. Rosebud also runs a tribal ranch that employs a small number of ranch workers.

Tribal government positions tend to be less stable than federal jobs for several reasons. Particularly for elected positions in tribal government, unemployment is a constant prospect because the terms of elected officials are only two years. A great deal of turnover in nonelected jobs follows each election as well. Furthermore, because of the uncertain revenue sources for the tribe, programs are often initiated but lose funding after two or three years and are discontinued.

Another common area of work is manual labor in construction, carpentry, and plumbing, and agricultural wage labor, which also tend to be temporary and seasonal. Manual labor positions include driving heavy machinery, masonry, electrical wiring, and twenty-four-hour security. In the 1980 U.S. census, 9 percent of the population of both Rosebud and Pine Ridge was engaged as laborers. Manual wage work is even more common for the parents of those I spoke with, with 27 percent reporting that during part or all of their childhood one or both of their parents had been engaged in manual wage work. There are also a small number of temporary seasonal jobs in border towns related to the tourist industry, such as maids in motels, restaurant dishwashers, and janitorial services.

The St. Francis Mission on Rosebud and the Holy Rosary Mission on Pine Ridge have also been important sources of wage work for Lakotas since these reservations were formed. Holy Rosary operates the Red Cloud Indian School in Pine Ridge and Our Lady of Lourdes school in Porcupine, which employ about one hundred fifty people. The St. Francis Mission concentrates its activities on the Little Sioux, a charitable organization dedicated to helping Lakotas, and employs about fifty people.

In the early 1990s, factory work and industrial jobs were limited to one shirt factory in Pine Ridge. At that time, the tribe was renovating an old moccasin factory and bringing in a business person to do saddles, boots, and other leather work there. A meat-packing plant had started in 1987 but had closed by 1989. The peak of industrial experiments came during the 1960s when War on Poverty programs funded the development of industrial parks in an effort to attract industry to American Indian reservations. The earliest factory in Pine Ridge was a cotton mattress factory that was instituted as part of the New Deal reforms of the 1930s and 1940s

(NA Pine Ridge B-33100-25-032 F13352-36-047). There were a fishhook factory, moccasin factory, arrow factory, and electronic circuit factory in Pine Ridge over the years, but all had closed by the early 1980s. Describing Rosebud, an Antelope woman said: "There have been some businesses that did all right here, but they closed them down. There was one that made all kinds of cabinets and things that were really good and are still in good shape, back in the '70s, but it closed. Then there was the electronics factory that made those microchips, but that closed too. Then there was this process that was used to turn a photograph into an oil painting, and that was really big around here for a while. So it would be interesting to know what goes on." Several of the operations in fact have been relocated to Mexico and other foreign countries.

Mainstream America's fascination with Indians has created its own set of economic opportunities: short-term wage work in the entertainment industry. Opportunities for acting in movies and television productions follow the cyclical interest of American popular culture in American Indians. During the years I lived on the reservations, the movies *Dances with Wolves, The Doors, Thunder Heart,* and *Lakota Woman* all generated local excitement and some local acting jobs, primarily as extras. One Porcupine woman recalls that her father took acting jobs in the 1950s and 1960s: "He was in about three or four movies. Like he was in *How the West Was Won,* and in *Katunka,* and *The Legend of the Sioux.* He made good money at that, and we all get a check now and then from the royalties." Another Rosebud woman has a nephew who made it into the circuit of Indian actors and who has earned $45,000 a year doing movies, while running a cattle business on the side, but his experience is the exception. An equal or greater number report being mistreated and being paid less than promised, and are generally disgruntled by their entertainment experience.

Migration to border towns and regional cities is another strategy for obtaining wage labor employment. Because the opportunities for work on the reservations continue to appear more limited than the opportunities off the reservation, particularly in large urban areas, many people have at least some period of wage work off the reservation. Of those I spoke with, 71 percent had either worked or accompanied a spouse to work off the reservation.

Wage work migration has historically responded to broader economic cycles. Wars, economic downturns, and industrialization all have had a direct impact on reservation communities. In boom times, government programs encourage training and relocation to off-reservation jobs.

As jobs become more scarce nationwide, opportunities for Lakota wage workers contract back to the reservation boundaries (Parman 1971:41).

Agricultural wage work was a mainstay of Lakota employment in the 1940s, 1950s and 1960s, until mechanization and changes in technology began replacing the need for farmhands. As the U.S. economy shifted to urban industrialization, government policy likewise encouraged native peoples to consider working in urban areas. If job opportunities were greater in cities, the thinking went, the economic burden on reservations would likely be less (Neils 1971:46–57). The federal Indian relocation program of the 1950s and 1960s provided support for travel to cities, job training, and initial household expenses. Like African-Americans from the rural South, some Lakotas were attracted to industrial labor in cities. In the 1980s, close to one-third of those on Rosebud Reservation had left for educational or vocational opportunities sometime in the last thirty years (Hargreaves & Chang 1989:12–13).

Lakotas choose to work and live in many different locations off the reservation. Denver, Minneapolis, and California are favored, but Lakotas have also worked in Texas, Arizona, New Mexico, Washington DC, and New York. Jobs held by those who spoke with me included university instructor, artist, airline attendant, janitor, truck driver, farmhand, mechanic, and business consultant. When their parents worked away from the reservation, their positions included railroad worker, fish hatchery worker, farmhand, janitor, mechanic, movie actor, nurse, and clerical worker.

Living in a city does not always mean that Lakotas have found more or better jobs, however. Because the ethnic hierarchy of the city labor market excludes Indian people from the economic mainstream, many families left one experience of poverty on the reservation for another in an urban area (Albers 1983:198, 201; Neils 1971:46–57, 91–104, 111–16). As the director of the Denver Indian Center observed, "People will drive up to the Indian Center straight here from their reservation with no money, no gas, no place to stay." Often no wage benefits derive from moving to the cities, either. In Denver, as on the reservation, the highest number (34 percent) of available jobs are in administrative support, including clerical (secretaries and typists), and service occupations (building cleaning, food services, and health services). Employment in regional cities also tends to be temporary or seasonal. For example, of the Native Americans employed in the Denver metropolitan area in 1979, only half worked for the entire year and a full third were employed twenty-six weeks or less (Colorado Department of Labor 1991). In the Denver area, of the 8,204 Native

Americans five years old or older living there in 1980, 32 percent had lived in a different state five years before.

Another longstanding employment possibility for the Lakotas is military service. The U.S. Army Indian Scouts received some of the earliest retirement benefits paid to reservation residents (South Dakota Historical Society 1890). Lakotas have fought in every U.S. war from World War I to Desert Storm. Traditions of military service have been handed down for generations within some families. One elderly woman from the Rosebud Reservation shares her husband's family history: "My husband was in World War II, and he had a brother in Korea, and his father was in World War I. It's kind of an interesting history. And this last brother was in Vietnam, so they really have served their country. The youngest brother's son was in Desert Storm, and he's still in the service." A man from Kyle has four brothers, and three of them "pensioned off the service. One was in the Burma War, and he got malaria and almost died there." Military service is among the most common forms of off-reservation work, particularly for young people. Lakotas have relatives stationed in Europe as well as in military posts across the United States. Some joined the military to acquire a few years of education and training. A Rosebud man who worked as an airline mechanic in California for many years explains, "I was in the navy, and that's how I got interested in engine maintenance work." Others are pursuing full careers in the military. As a Porcupine man puts it: "I finished high school and there weren't any jobs for me to do as a permanent full-time worker, so I decided to join the military. There are only two reasons you go into the army. Either you want to make a career out of it, or because you don't know what else to do, and that was me, I didn't know what else to do."

World Economy in the Workplace

The broader economy imposes demands on all these wage labor opportunities, although Lakotas have unique methods of interpreting and abating those demands. In an area of high unemployment, Lakota workers have little or no power to influence the requirements of their employers. The hours, duration, and pay of their work, and mobility within the workplace, largely suit the employer. Most Lakota employees must work the hours set by the employer or risk getting fired. A Lakota woman describes her seasonal job as a hotel maid in Interior: "In the summer I was working in housekeeping, making five dollars an hour, usually about thirty-five hours a week, but it was getting to be more at the end. I'd be on my way home from a long day looking forward to a day off and before I'd get in the door the phone would ring with my boss asking if I could come in in the morning, because they laid someone else off. And if you say no, then you're the next one to go, so I was working all the time lately. My job will be ended now, in the wintertime."

A woman from Oglala had a similar experience of having to take on more and more of the burden of a temporary job: "The last job I had was being a 1990 census worker. They paid $5.65 an hour plus 20 cents a mile for gas. I did it before, in 1980, and they really paid good then. I made like $1,800 a month that time. But this time they didn't pay good, plus the people didn't know what they were doing. So more and more people dropped out until I was the only one left for the whole rez, and then I fell sick in August and also quit, so I don't know if anyone ever finished. I did about half the rez just myself. We started out with five workers, and they all dropped but me. The hardest part was budgeting the gas I'd need for the week before I got the next paycheck."

A common frustration is the lack of control over working hours. A man from Rosebud told me: "I'm real tired of working for people, being at their discretion for whatever they want you to do. With consulting or my own business, I think I could work out my own schedule, and work out how hard I have to work. Making enough to be comfortable without having to work forty or fifty hours a week and maintain your standard of living, start to enjoy what you've worked for instead of running off to work or whatever. So to be self-employed or self-sufficient is my goal." A woman from Antelope has a similar view on arbitrary working hours: "I'd like to create institutions where people are allowed the freedom to do their work and when the work is done, you call it a day, rather than this notion that you have to work to the sacrifice of all other things in life, your family and your community obligations. Institutions are just too rigid about when people have to be there physically, and neglect the fact that there are times people won't be productive under that system."

Poor working conditions are another source of dissatisfaction for Lakota wage laborers. Boredom and negative health effects plague many workers. A woman from Wanbli recalls:

> I used to work for that arrow factory when it was still going up here. Arrows, arrows every day, it was really boring. I had to make about two thousand arrows a day. I got paid $380 a week if I made about two thousand arrows every day. I used a machine to put the arrows together. There were quite a few of us working over there then. My sister was a supervisor. There were a lot of district people that got jobs out of the factory. They had three shifts going, from 7 A.M. to 4, 4 to 11, and 11 P.M. to 7 A.M., so they really made use of that place. They were selling arrows all over, I guess, like

at KMart and sporting stores. The glue we had to use was this permabond stuff, and I used to get asthma attacks bad off that stuff. I had to go to Pine Ridge to get shots to help me breathe, but I was getting sick off that glue all that time.

A Manderson woman worked for the electronics plant in 1977: "I was only about twenty-four back then. We got minimum wages, and it was a boring job. You sat there wrapping these spools with wire all day, but we didn't have anything else to do so everyone tried to work there. I'd say there were about twenty people who worked there each shift, two shifts a day. I think part of why it closed was no one wanted to show up for work. Those spools were around here for a long time after that, you see them lying in the ditches and rolling in the parking lots."

One striking thing about the unemployed Lakotas who spoke with me is the number who had been severely injured on the job. A Kyle woman refers to several work-related health problems: "I made moccasins for three years, but I got blisters from the dye on the moccasins. Then I drove a Head Start bus, but I got a sunstroke and had to quit." An elderly man from Rosebud experienced a horrifying work accident: "I worked for the government for sixteen years, doing all kinds of maintenance work, until they had me blow myself up. They told me to cut open this tank, but they didn't tell me the tank was heated, so as I cut into it, it blew up. They called my brother and told him to come over because I had about two hours to live. I had burns over 70 percent of my body and some broken bones, and lost a disc out of my back. After that I got a few weeks of workman's compensation and then I was laid off." A mechanic in his early forties reports: "I got hurt on the job. I had to have my wrist taken out and an artificial wrist put in." Another man was hit on the head by a two-by-four during a renovation job, could not work, and had no income for six weeks.

Continuously low wages are another source of frustration for Lakota wage laborers. Relatively few positions offer significant opportunities for promotion and salary increases. A woman from Rosebud, exhausted after making minimal wages as a secretary for almost twenty years, wryly comments: "I've always worked. After I finished school [ninth grade], I was here for two months, then went to Pierre to take the [General Educational Development, or GED] test, and then I got a job right away, so ever since then I've worked. I keep asking my husband, when can I ever quit work? I'm going to die working [laughs]." In the 1990 census, the mean individual salary or wage income was $13,544 in Pine Ridge and $15,297 in Rosebud. The poverty line in the United States for a family of four at that time was $14,750 (*New York Times*, 7/26/93, A8c1). This poverty-level income does not go unnoticed. A woman from Rosebud observes: "The way things are around here, most people get minimum wage. The minimum keeps going up, but you can't keep up with it." A woman from Pine Ridge worked for the same non-governmental organization for nearly twenty years but had her salary frozen for seven of those years and is now just beginning to make $20,000 per year. "They came back after the board meeting and said my salary wasn't frozen anymore," she told me, "and I was getting a cost of living increase, a whole 3 percent. Then I was still mad, because at that point I wanted them to keep me frozen so I could tell them, 'I quit!' "

The level of specialization most commonly associated with promotion and financial advancement in the mainstream economy is seldom a possibility for reservation residents. Because wage labor positions are rarely permanent, secure, or full-time, Lakotas often see their work experiences through the prism of a wide variety of economic activities rather than in terms of a particular specialization. Most Lakotas during their lives participate in a number of forms of wage labor. As a woman from St. Francis reports, "I've worked for virtually every institution here on the reservation." Another woman recites her experiences as a dental therapist, a director of a nonprofit organization, a Head Start worker, and a tribal employee.

The scarcity of workplace specialization is related to some extent to education. Many Lakotas attribute their lack of job or salary advancement to their education. Although the level of educational attainment is increasing with each generation, there is still a high dropout rate. According to the 1990 census, for those sixty years or older, only 4 percent in Rosebud and 14 percent in Pine Ridge had a high school diploma or equivalency, and 47 percent in Pine Ridge and 53 percent in Rosebud had less than a ninth-grade education. In contrast, more than half those twenty-five years or older had at least a high school diploma. Few Lakotas, however, have pursued higher education. In the 1990 census, fewer than 4 percent on either reservation had earned a college degree or undertook graduate-level studies.

Economic factors account for the lack of education for some Lakotas. Some leave school early to have children and marry. In the past, when most Lakota families were engaged in agricultural wage work, some parents could not afford to send their children to school in town. An elderly woman from Antelope ended her education in the seventh grade when her parents could no longer pay eight dollars a week for her sister and her to live in town during the school year. When parents were working in fields and on ranches, children were expected to help. Children would also miss school when their parents migrated seasonally for agricultural work. An Oglala woman recalls: "I went to Holy Rosary, up to the ninth grade. At that point my dad was broke and I needed clothes to go to school, so I dropped out and we went to Wyoming to earn our winter clothes picking potatoes." A Lakota elementary teacher observes that parents continue to move for jobs, still interrupting the educational progress of students in her school.

Other people attribute their difficulty qualifying for well-paying jobs to the type of education they received in Indian boarding schools. Rather than academic excellence, these boarding schools emphasized training for menial wage work (Adams 1995:22; Littlefield 1993:43). A woman from Kyle notes that when her mother went to school, "she learned to cook and sew, more of the vocational skills." Most Lakotas over age forty spent some or all of their school years living in either a BIA or a Christian boarding school, deliberately separated from the "corrupting" influences of their unassimilated parents (Adams 1995:22–23; Child 1998:43; Ellis 1996:3–5; Standing Bear 1928:123–32). Boarding schools had farms, orchards, machine shops, and sewing rooms where students produced items that subsidized the schools' operating costs. Such labor was couched as educational experience. Littlefield has argued that this was a conscious decision on the part of the federal administrators, in order to create a core of Indian wage laborers (1996:100–102). An elder Rosebud woman agrees: "The same government that provided vocational oriented education now expects reservation residents to live on wage work. They did us a big service in boarding school, teaching us discipline and how to work hard, but they really let us down on the education part, so no matter how hard we worked, we weren't prepared to compete with the outside world with our intellects. That's still going on now, you know. They train our people to be dependent and not know how to compete in the system."

The impositions of the world economy are gradually becoming more apparent through the educational requirements for reservation work. Most Lakotas I spoke with feel that the overall level of education needed to find jobs is increasing. A high school diploma or GED used to be adequate for any government, tribal, or nonprofit organization position. Now two-year college degrees are being required for the same jobs. A woman from Rosebud in her thirties feels her prospects for job advancement are dim: "I think school is the most important for the young people to make it. I'm kind of getting up there in age, but when you just go to ninth grade, it doesn't hit you until you're almost forty and it hits you that you can't make any kind of money unless you have some sort of schooling. And anymore when you apply for a job they ask you what kind of schooling and if you have any credits. I found that out in just the last couple months looking for another kind of job, and that's the first thing they ask is if you have any other kind of schooling. The secretarial things I know is stuff I learned on the job." A woman from Oglala agrees: "There aren't many jobs around here now, and you need at least two years of college or a degree to get them. Education is a big thing now. It's important, and that will get harder on people because it's also expensive." Lakotas today emphasize the value of education for their children. As a mother from Pine Ridge declares: "My son wants to go to VoTech, but I want him to do something broader than just diesel mechanics, like engineering."

The educational system seems designed to attract the best and the brightest Lakotas away from the reservation. For the most part, professional degrees such as those in business, law, social work, or medicine, or technical vocational certificates such as those needed by beauticians and mechanics, have to be obtained off the reservation. Those willing to pursue higher education to improve their economic opportunities must be willing to leave their reservation community.

Interestingly, it is as difficult for highly trained professionals as unskilled workers to find satisfactory employment on the reservations. Lakotas who obtain advanced degrees or are interested in professional advancement encounter a glass ceiling on the reservation. With the limited number of academic positions at the tribal colleges and the equally limited number of non-governmental organizations to be director of, along with the politics and gridlock of government jobs and tribal offices, many people in their late thirties and early forties feel there is no choice but to work outside the reservation for at least some length of time. In 1990, the occupational category with the highest percentage of unemployed in Pine Ridge's Shannon County was technical and managerial professionals (35.6 percent) (South Dakota Department of Labor 1991).

Lakota Culture in the Workplace

Despite the difficulties surrounding wage and professional work, reservation residents are able to create some economic space to avoid unfavorable employment conditions. In such a tight job market, one might expect to find a Lakota workforce willing to do anything to keep a job. This is not the case in Pine Ridge and Rosebud, however. I was amazed at the ease with which Lakotas quit their jobs. Of a group of ten Lakota men and women with whom I kept ongoing contact, seven resigned and changed positions within an eight-month period. It is often hard to assess when employment termination is a voluntary pursuit of cultural ideals or is involuntary but rationalized as all for the best. People rarely contribute anecdotes about their own shortcomings or possible legitimate justifications for their removal from a position, leading a listener to assess the reports of the misdeeds of others with a grain of salt.

Facets of Lakota culture are used to explain or justify leaving the workforce. For example, many Lakotas today, as in earlier years, view life as a path that is revealed through dreams, visions, and other signs (DeMallie 1984:83–87; W. Powers 1975:57; Walker 1980:79, 85; Young Bear and Theisz 1994:79–80). Such a cultural disposition was responsible for the departure of an Oglala woman from the workforce: "I worked for the Postal Service as a replacement, but my boss, I caught her for embezzlement. Like in Indian way, they say everything happens two times. So I kept working though, and she got laid off, so I got another boss. Then she started doing things out of the way, so I decided I better resign, because this is a telltale sign. I had nightmares that this postal inspector was standing over me and I was lying on the floor and he was threatening me, and so I said 'That's a sign I have to resign,' because I don't want to be a part of anything she is doing." Another woman accounts for her unemployment after complications from surgery by claiming: "There must be a reason. I must be meant to do something else."

Other Lakotas express unwillingness to continue with jobs that they are philosophically in conflict with. It is difficult for Lakotas to be part of a system that is failing to serve, or is actually harming, their community. For these individuals, the motivation to work is less a paycheck than a desire to help their neighbors, relatives, and friends. For example, the health care needs of the communities far exceed the resources of the Indian Health Service (IHS). This problem causes considerable stress to Lakotas employed by IHS who are genuinely concerned about serving others, as a former IHS worker recounts:

> IHS Mental Health was so rigid, all they cared about was being there in the office from nine to five, not whether you were actually helping people with their problems. I don't ever want to get stuck in a job like that again. Once I went through family counseling and understood how to confront my problems, I had to leave my job at Mental Health, because they made me the scapegoat for the real problems I was confronting them with. The doctors felt uncomfortable with me because they said I was angry, rather than looking at their own role in the problems, and they labeled me a troublemaker. So I knew it was time to leave. I was never so happy as when my supervisor said I was on call that night and I said, "No, I'm not, I've resigned." I decided then never to get embedded in that kind of institution again.

Lakota culture also injects itself into the economic system in the form of the extended family, a center of support and duty. The attitudes and values of the larger community play a key role in both defining economic "need" and providing additional safety nets during hard times. On Pine Ridge and Rosebud, these values encourage acts of generosity, sharing, and self-sacrifice for the good of the community. According to Lakota values, people are defined by their relatives, rather than by their occupation or their material wealth (One Feather 1974:22–23; Walker 1982:5–6; Young Bear and Theisz 1994:57).

The availability of some form of public assistance, however limited, combined with support from the extended family, has made it possible for Lakotas to leave jobs that are regarded as too onerous. According to the 1990 census, 45 percent of Pine Ridge households and 47 percent of Rosebud households receive public assistance. With limited wage labor opportunities, welfare support has become a critical resource, particularly for women with children and the elderly. The amounts of this form of support are minimal, however. In 1993, a woman with three children was eligible for $329 to $450 per month in AFDC payments. In 1999, a woman with three children was eligible for approximately $350 per month under Temporary Assistance to Needy Families (TANF). The TANF program, implemented in 1997, is of tremendous concern to Lakotas. Although the five-year lifetime limit is not currently being enforced, the insistence that welfare recipients find wage work in order to receive welfare benefits has far-reaching consequences in small rural villages that lack a large pool of even menial jobs (Pickering 2000).

Some Lakotas, like some other Americans outside the reservations, feel that public assistance creates disincentives for engaging in wage work and welcome the changes presented by TANF. A woman working in Mission explains: "It's working people who have a harder time making their payments. The system is really set up to work for the people on welfare and against the people who are working. If you're working, you have to pay a third of your income to HUD for housing, you don't qualify for Food Stamps or energy assistance, plus you have all the costs of babysitting and gas and cars. Whereas people who aren't working may even have a negative rent, with all the social services and economic supports at hand." Some feel the social safety net has simply been too supportive. As a woman from Wanbli remarks: "[TANF] will get these young men off their behinds and get them to work." A disgruntled Oglala mother exclaims: "I have three children, and the two boys live with me still. They both are not even working. One's twenty-nine years old. I can't even get away from him. My son says, 'You don't like me,' but I say 'If I nag you, it's because I want you to get out and work, get a training or something, it's not that I hate you.'"

Conflicts also exist between Lakota views on family values and the wage-labor workplace. Pressures are being exerted for new forms of child care as more extended family members enter the workforce. At the same time, however, some Lakotas are unhappy with the lack of time and attention working parents have for their children. One community school on the Pine Ridge Reservation tried an alternative schedule of "four days a week, then tutoring in the afternoons. I think it's good because they get the parents involved in the teaching from 3:30 to 5:30, to sit with their kids in the classes. But you hear the parents complaining because now they lack one day of a babysitter and food on Friday, rather than looking at what it's providing for their kids."

Others use Lakota family values to improve their job opportunities. For example, Lakota families draw on family ties to locate and hire co-workers, a practice defined by mainstream principles as nepotism. But with a limited pool of workers with special skills, hiring a relative is often necessary. A woman from Pine Ridge describes a typical work scenario involving family: "They wouldn't hire one of my sisters in the finance department because they said it would be nepotism, although they hired my other sister later, in a different department though. She already had a lot of experience in that area." In other instances, having a relative hired helps others get a foot in the door for other jobs. "My wife got a job as a teacher," a Rosebud man recalls. "The superintendent asked me to fix a few things, and then asked me to come on as an industrial art teacher. I ended up teaching for eighteen years."

Lakotas commonly feel that people with high-level positions with the tribe or the BIA have the most control over who fills government and bureaucratic openings and that "they only help their own friends and relatives." Within the tribal government the chances of getting a job improve if one has a relative in office. Individual decisions about pursuing elected office are fraught with implications for relatives of a candidate. A woman from Rosebud reports, "My uncle was going to run for office, and I was going to try to work for him if he got in at the tribal office, but he decided not to run."

The support of the *tiyóšpaye* extends off the reservation. Distant relatives free Lakotas to seek employment in a new location. People repeatedly mention staying with Lakota relatives and close friends in cities where they are looking for summer jobs or permanent work, working at a temporary job, or attending college or vocational school. For example, one woman's son was laid off from his construction job for the winter, so he went to stay with his grandmother on another reservation where they needed truck drivers; he was employed there for the winter months. Another woman's son went to Portland, Oregon, where an aunt lived, in order to seek summer employment.

Lakota family values can also have a negative effect on the workplace. Customarily difficult working conditions become even more difficult if a relative turns into a troublesome coworker. A woman from Pine Ridge recounts an instance in which she rode with her sister-in-law, a coworker, to attend a two-day meeting. Her sister-in-law went out partying and never picked her up for the meeting, so their employer charged them personally for their hotel rooms: "I said, 'I'm not paying back the money for the motel, because I went in good faith, and if you'd told me you weren't going to go, I would've driven myself.' And it's harder where she's my sister-in-law. If it was anyone else, I probably would have held her up to the director, but because it was her, I tried to keep it in. But it hurt my credibility, and when she didn't take responsibility, I really got mad, but it made me uncomfortable to rat on her. So I had to pay back the room money."

Family values and cultural ties also impose obligations that often conflict with economic pressures to leave the reservation to find work. From the sweeping perspective of the world economy, jobs are interchangeable. Members of local Lakota households, however, weigh the opportunities of labor migration against the loss of their cultural community. Lakotas who work off the reservation essentially leave a community where being Indian is the norm for a place where Indians are mostly invisible. The possibility of higher wages is not necessarily enough to compensate for that loss of identity and community. A woman from Rosebud told me, "I went to Rapid City, but I came back because I didn't like the city, even though the wages were about four dollars an hour more up there." As mentioned, the shock of transition from reservation to city life can be softened by relatives who already live in the cities. Other ways to lessen the loss of cultural ties are urban Indian community centers and events such as powwows that have been developed by reservation migrants.

Obligations to family members on the reservation are often cited as the reason people return to Pine Ridge and Rosebud. Illness, a death in the family, or a call for help in a family enterprise are all important motivations to return to the reservation. A woman from Oglala recalls, "[My husband and I] were in California four years, and then they wrote and told us his mother had cancer so we had to come back."

Wage work and the imposition of demands from the world economy also threaten to undermine the Lakotas' long-standing ideal of support and respect toward elders. According to Lakota religious tradition, one of the two rules brought by White Buffalo Calf Woman to the Lakotas was to respect one's elders (DeMallie 1984:81–82; One Feather 1974: 21). Incorporation into a capitalist economy has strained this rule in several ways. First, the economic and social demands of mainstream society are placing more responsibility on younger, middle-aged people who are able to move from the Lakota world to the non-Indian world more easily than their elders. The aunt of a forty-year-old Manderson woman suggested that her niece be the chair of their peer lending group because she was "education wise." As the niece describes it: "Technically, all the other people in the group are older than I am, so I shouldn't be in a position to tell them what to do, but they said I should go ahead, because even though I'm the chairman of the group, they can still scold me. Now there is lots of responsibility on the youngest people. In the old days, you never had responsibility until you were old enough to handle it."

Second, the need for young people to gain work experience conflicts with the traditional Lakota attitude that ability comes only with age (Hassrick 1964:16–17; Walker 1982:180 n. 65). For example, young people in their twenties find themselves at the greatest disadvantage in looking for full-time work. As a twenty-five-year-old man from Wanbli laments: "They look at my age, and say I can't do anything. For my age group, there aren't many opportunities for jobs or anything. That's why a lot of them try to go to college here. Or then they'll decide to take time off for a year and that turns into many years without them really doing anything, but it's hard for them to get from kick-back mode into a degree again."

Third, generational differences in workplace experiences create conflicts between young and old over how to approach difficult work conditions. Some younger Lakotas express frustration with the older generation for accepting workplace mistreatment, seeing their acquiescence as evidence of their having internalized years of oppression by the mainstream society. Older Lakotas were indeed more hesitant to complain to me about wages and other work conditions than the younger generation. A Kyle man in his sixties explains his attitude toward work: "One year our wages went up, then the school went bankrupt so it was back down to $4 an hour. I never worked for high wages before, so it didn't bother me, but the others really complained. Now the contract is up to $7.88. Some get $8 and $10, so they're satisfied now. If you fight for more wages, and then have no job, where does that get you?"

The Special Case of Non-Governmental Organizations

One source of employment on the reservations, particularly for Lakota directors and managers, is a wide array of nonprofit, non-governmental organizations (NGOs). The workplace experiences of Lakota employees at Lakota-created nonprofit organizations throw into relief the interplay between demands of the world economy and the beliefs and values of their indigenous culture. Because NGOs are formed to address various issues and provide services specific to the social and cultural needs of the Lakota community, these organizations respond to and reflect certain Lakota values. But because NGOs are subject to outside legal regulations and the structures of nonprofit organizations, they also respond to and reflect aspects of the world economy and the broader U.S. political system.

Although no single NGO provides jobs to more than a handful of individuals, the cumulation of all the NGOs operating on the two reservations constitutes a significant sector of the employment pool, following federal and tribal government jobs. Among the NGOs operating on Pine Ridge and Rosebud are Oglala Lakota College, Sinte Gleska University, Dakota Plains Legal Service, White Buffalo Calf Women's Society, Sacred Shawl Women's Society, Sue Ann Big Crow Youth Center, Project Phoenix, the Lakota Fund, and Sicangu Enterprise Center.

Lakota-based NGOs are created in the belief that only indigenously controlled institutions can be fully responsive to Lakota needs and concerns. As social and living conditions on the reservations continue to change, families are often caught up more with day-to-day issues of economic survival than with perpetuating Lakota traditions. Lakota NGOs have become a new mechanism for promoting Lakota culture and tradition. The Sicangu Youth Camp, for example, is a week-long outdoor camp supported by the tribe for children in Rosebud. Children learn about Lakota values, history, arts and crafts, and ceremonies such as the *huká* or ritual adoption. NGO workers try hard to meet the special needs of Indian communities. A woman from Rosebud provides seminars on positive self-image and reinforcement: "I would ask, 'What kinds of things make you feel good to be native?' People would say things like the smell of fry bread, Indian jewelry, or beadwork."

Both reservations have tribal colleges that offer a full range of two-year associate degrees, four-year bachelor's degrees, and a small number of graduate programs. The tribal colleges attempt to meet the special cultural needs of the Lakota community while complying with the requirements of the broader, nonreservation society. In addition to mainstream departments such as mathematics, computer science, and business, they offer courses in history, government, and culture that are unique to the Lakota experience. This focus provides the opportunity for salaried positions for members of the local community who are outstanding Lakota speakers, part of historically significant families, or firsthand participants in the struggles for tribal self-determination and civil rights.

Lakotas do not agree on the quality of education offered at the tribal colleges. On the one hand, the tribal colleges make higher education potentially available to a much larger portion of the reservation population, particularly women with children. Tribal college courses are attended by a range of individuals, from those immediately out of high school to those making career changes in their forties and even fifties. The tribal colleges are also an increasingly important alternative for the large number of young people who try an off-reservation college and find the environment overwhelming, alienating, or irrelevant to their intellectual, social, and cultural interests.

Others feel that tribal colleges meet neither Lakota standards nor mainstream standards. One man from Rosebud who had studied economics and business in California told me: "Now they call Sinte Gleska a university, but it's only for public relations. The students aren't getting a university education, and if they are ever in a situation where real university graduates are involved, they won't be able to compete." Alternatively, several women from the Rosebud Reservation perceive that the tribal college is perpetuating the same form and substance of education as any white, mainstream college. "The college isn't living up to its mission as a tribal college," one woman remarks. "They're just the same as all the other institutions out there, not meeting the needs of Indian students."

Because of the tensions between local and national expectations, working for Lakota NGOs is often stressful. Those who have been employed for a long time by local NGOs experience mental fatigue from unrelenting exposure to the most difficult reservation problems and constant criticism from external forces monitoring the NGO's performance. As a woman from Rosebud observes about NGO workers: "The problem is, after a while, they lose that human quality and become really negative about the population. It seems like the people really burn out." Job insecurity can add to the stress of NGO workers. Unlike federal and tribal positions, which are relatively permanent, jobs with NGOs tend to be highly unstable and uncertain because the organizations depend on grants from various sources for their payrolls. People working for local NGOs also must navigate the contradictions between the difficult conditions in their Lakota communities and the affluence of organizations and foundations that supply financial and technical support. A woman from Rosebud shares her experience: "I just got back from this Ms. Foundation conference on economic development and rural community development. They had it at this Pitney-Bowes retreat place in Atlanta. I kept saying it didn't feel right to be there, because it was really nice, fancy and all, but they kept telling me 'It's okay, you deserve it. Just think of every time you use one of their machines you are paying for this place.' So I figure it's okay."

The double-edged sword of federal funding confronts many Lakota organizations. Ideally, Lakota NGOs would choose to function without any federal funding, because of the strings of control that accompany federal dollars. One primary negative aspect of accepting federal funds is the tremendous amount of paperwork needed to comply with reporting and audit requirements. An employee at one Lakota alcohol treatment center describes this tension: "The problem with taking federal money is they want to know everything, but then you become like mainstream treatment, where they focus on paperwork all the time and don't spend time with the clients' individual problems." Despite this problem, Lakota organizations face the fact that most of the grant programs available to fund their activities are federal.

Lakota organizations can apply to the local Catholic church for funds to support education and charitable activities on the reservation. "The mission makes grants to help people start businesses," a man from Rosebud assures me. "They would just like you to put somebody to work." Those who receive aid from the St. Francis Mission are sometimes unhappy with the church's social and financial strings, however. A woman from St. Francis observes: "It's hard to be involved with these organizations, even if I agree with them, when those priests and nuns are in there trying to control things." Another St. Francis woman comments:

> The church really makes us frustrated because on the one hand they give us financial support, but on the other hand they want to watch over every penny. I was a religion teacher for the mission for seven years, and they watched over everything, down to how many number 1 and number 2 pencils you got, until you didn't have time for the teaching they were so worried about finances. Now they only give us portions of the grant as they see fit, so twice we've been late with payroll because they didn't make the transfer in time. That is just too frustrating. Sometimes I think the Father thinks this is his project. We just got another grant from an outside organization, and the church took that money and put it into CDs, as if it was theirs or something.

A man from St. Francis sees a larger problem in accepting money from the church: "Resentments against institutions are harder to overcome than resentments against individuals. Placing this organization in a position of being solely funded by the church raises all these issues: boarding school, religious oppression, control of the community."

Private foundations are another potential source for NGO funding. Lakota NGOs are funded by many national foundations, such as the Kellogg, Robert Wood Johnson, Northwest Area, and Turner Foundations. To receive donations from private foundations or from individuals interested in getting a tax deduction, Lakota organizations must conform to the institutional and paperwork requirements necessary to obtain tax-exempt status from the Internal Revenue Service. Filing the forms to request tax-exempt status often keeps sound local organizations from getting off the ground for years. A tax-exempt organization must have formal documents indicating that the entity is structured in a Western model for conducting business, such as articles of association or articles of incorporation and by-laws. The individuals serving on the board of directors need to be listed, a requirement that implies that every nonprofit organization must have such a board.

One difficulty noted by several NGO directors is providing the evidence to national funders that the objectives of a proposed project were accomplished. Maintaining books and records is essential to meeting the demands of outside funders. Many Lakota NGOs do not keep the types of files and statistics that are commonplace outside the reservation, however. A Lakota NGO board member explains: "According to the [program funder], we don't keep detailed records of our meetings. I don't know anyone who actually wants to keep that type of records. Anything we do we just relay it back to the main office, give a copy of any document or anything they do so they can keep it on their system."

If outside evaluators are used to assess a project, they often do not understand the nature of those culturally based services that were undocumented. For example, several organizations work to find culturally based alcohol treatment approaches. Lakota individuals trained in alcohol counseling with sensitivity to the stresses and conditions of Indian life are in great demand. Drawing on aspects of Lakota culture to help native alcoholics recover and heal, a substance abuse counselor took his patients to sweat lodge ceremonies and included them in community events as part of their treatment, mentoring them in their rediscovery of sober life. These activities, however, were not viewed as valid clinical hours when the program was evaluated by the national foundation funding the NGO.

The support of capitalist institutions such as insurance companies also limits the methodology and style of operations that Lakota entities can adopt. A local organization that advocates a culturally sensitive approach to alcohol treatment found that its potential clients were constrained by their insurance companies. The director of one of these centers shares her frustration: "The insurance companies won't accept traditional services as the basis for a claim. They demand an accounting to the penny and insist that time be spent with a 'qualified' clinical psychologist in order to provide payment for alcohol treatment." The fact that there are only a handful of Lakota individuals who have completed the clinical training insisted on by the mainstream health industry thus becomes a barrier to the Lakota community's defining its own path to recovery.

The wholesale incorporation of programs from non-Indian organizations is another point of contention. In the area of alcohol treatment, Lakota community members debate whether non-Indian approaches to treatment and family are appropriate or effective for Lakota alcoholics and their families. Although Alcoholics Anonymous works for some, others see it as incompatible with the tiny reservation communities where anonymity is virtually impossible.

Others feel there needs to be a truly Lakota approach to alcohol treatment, with Lakota counselors an essential part of making treatment effective. A woman from Antelope asserts: "I hope I can go back to school at some point and develop an alternative approach to that of AA, because there are a lot of their principles that I disagree with. Like for me, my children live with me, and they would say that's enabling, but I don't think there is anything wrong with that. If I put them out, how is that going to be any better for them? And this way I'm with my granddaughter and can help my children with their plans."

Capital and Culture in Small Business

A small number of Lakotas own small businesses. According to the 1990 census, only 5 percent of Rosebud and 7 percent of Pine Ridge households reported nonfarm self-employment income, most related to small business operations, with a mean amount of $8,523 in Rosebud and $11,488 in Pine Ridge. A related study of small businesses and microenterprises at Pine Ridge indicates that the average annual income of small business households was $26,627 with $11,833 net business income (Mushinski & Pickering 1996:161). Convenience and gas stores, car repair shops, restaurants, home repair and renovation, home and office cleaning services, office computer and management services, and other consulting services are the most common forms of small business. Of the small businesses operating on the reservations, less than one-third had storefronts or offices with signs to indicate the name of the business.

There are fewer small businesses on the reservations than the local populations can support. In Pine Ridge, with a population approaching thirty thousand, there are fewer than fifty small businesses across the reservation. Less than half of them are Indian owned. Only one out of five small businesses is predicted to be still operating after three years.

As disconcerting as the figures might seem, they reflect signs of positive growth. There are now more small businesses in absolute number and more Indian-owned businesses than in the 1960s. Indian-owned small business played a limited role on the reservations before 1970. For example, in 1917, there were only four traders licensed to do business on the Rosebud Reservation, and none of them was Lakota (FARC Rosebud A-436, 8/23/17:28). A number of non-Indian businessmen married Lakota women and raised children on the reservation who ultimately inherited their businesses, however.

Lakota small business people must learn to navigate both the mores of Lakota culture and the demands of the world economy. They are caught between the conflicting expectations of market exchange relations and Lakota social relations. Every day they are expected to embody the best of both worlds.

Commercial Expectations

Lakota small business people are expected by the non-Indians they deal with to conform to the mold of a commercial enterprise operating outside the reservation, expressing efficiency and financial acumen. They are also expected by outsiders to possess the demeanor, goals, and experience of non-Lakota business people, including financial collateral, credit history, work history, educational background, and financial recordkeeping. Outside lenders, suppliers, and competitors require from them the kinds of paperwork and business plans that are taken for granted in the mainstream economy. Because few Lakota small businesses operate in this economic arena, special requirements or expectations are sometimes imposed on them. For example, non-native suppliers who are unfamiliar with and therefore uncertain about dealing with a native business person might require that all invoices be paid on time, every time. "I've met business people that only see an Indian," a Pine Ridge businessman reflects, "and sometimes I have to be lenient to get them to look at this person in a different way so they'll take your product seriously, be ready to go the extra mile so your product is not on the bottom shelf, straighten out the boxes, show you really care about your product."

Lakota small businesses on the reservations compete with comparable businesses on both regional and local levels for a limited number of customers. Like small businesses everywhere, Lakota small businesses must compete with multinational chains such as Wal-Mart and Safeway in the larger towns on the borders and in regional cities. The increasing mobility of the reservation population makes trips to such regional cities and border towns easier and easier; Lakota small businesses thus sometimes have great difficulty keeping their customer base on the reservation. For example, a local special-order T-shirt business in Mission has trouble competing with prices in regional cities, especially for rush orders when the business has to buy its supplies at full price from local border town stores. "A lot of times they'll tell us it's too high and they'll just go to Rapid City to order them," I was told. Furthermore, a lack of competition among off-reservation suppliers and limited local consumer markets depress the profits that Lakota small business producers can demand.

Locally, Lakota small businesses compete with other Indian-owned and non-Indian-owned enterprises on the reservation. The relatively low number of reservation consumers presents an acute problem of direct competition among small businesses. Once a Lakota business becomes successful in a particular local market, it is common for other community members to open competing businesses in the exact same market. As a Pine Ridge businessman recalls: "I had a café for five years and did a good business. Then seven others came and went, trying to compete for the same market. Rather than finding an open area, they all jump in where there's already a successful business, and then neither one can make a living." A computer instructor from Pine Ridge is particularly aware of the problem of new competition: "There's enough work in this area to keep a person busy, but every time I pass someone in my class, I'm essentially working myself out of a job. Granted, there are some higher-level computer tasks that still need to be done and still need programming, but the bulk of what I do is application work, using software or teaching software, so I really haven't gotten to the level where I'd like to be, teaching programming and systems analysis. If we were ever to get to that level, then I certainly would have to fight the competition. Right now I think there is enough work."

Rather than adjust to new competition, existing small businesses often close down when a new store opens. A woman from Kyle feels this common reaction and decision needs to be reconsidered: "That store that's going out of business here, after that new one opened up, you know, they could rent their space out, because there is hardly any business space available in town here, or they could do something about their business and try to stay in business, like try to advertise or rethink which items to sell. They should change their standpoint rather than just go under because a new situation has occurred."

Most Lakota business people try to adhere to the basic management principles of good business, minimizing costs and maximizing productivity and profits. Many Lakotas who follow mainstream management principles feel that they are essential to the success of a business, Lakota-owned or not. A St. Francis businessman concludes: "The bottom line for business is you need the same basic tools regardless of where you are." A Pine Ridge businessman argues that management principles in fact are at the heart of why Lakota businesses frequently have trouble getting off the ground: "The problem with asking business people about their own businesses is they tend to blame someone else, the tribe, the suppliers, a conspiracy out there against them, but in fact they're just bad managers."

Lakota owners of small businesses face tremendous pressure to leave the reservations in order to pursue specialized training and certification. Small business people such as computer consultants, mental health counselors, and lawyers often have a special expertise acquired through higher education and training, much of which can be obtained only at colleges off the reservation. Other small business people emphasize the importance of on-the-job training and prior business ventures, sometimes off the reservation, for gaining skills needed to run a successful business. A Pine Ridge businessman who has worked in five different states claims: "All the different jobs I've had have helped me with this business. Being able to work with people especially." A St. Francis businessman observes: "I left the rez for twenty-five years to develop my business skills. I worked in and started businesses all over." Another Pine Ridge businessman advises: "I think young people need to leave the rez to learn about how things are run, because if they don't, then they'll always be at a disadvantage in competing with others who have had that experience and know how the system works."

Lakota Expectations

Staying competitive can be challenging if the limited profit margins of a small business are used to meet culturally dictated social obligations. Local communities expect Lakota business people to express such traditional values as generosity, being a good relative, and taking responsibility for the group. Community members with legitimate needs remind Lakota business people, "I'm your relative," thus laying claim to the financial support that local social relations require of extended family and fictive kin.

Those Lakota owners of small businesses who resist redistributing their business profits to their extended kin are viewed as taking advantage of the community in order to enrich themselves. For example, community members regularly criticized the Lakota owner of a convenience store for charging high prices and paying low wages rather than sharing his wealth with his Lakota customers and employees. The egalitarian premise of the reservation economy is that everyone will stay within the same general realm of financial well-being through reciprocity and redistribution and no one will be substantially better off than anyone else (Hassrick 1964:37; Walker 1982:65).

Any incipient wealth being accumulated by the small business people on the reservation directly challenges these egalitarian principles. As a result, community attitudes are often negative toward Indian small business people. According to one St. Francis businessman: "The population on the rez still looks at entrepreneurs as being better off, even than other working elements of the society, like the school superintendent or the BIA employee. Businessmen are not a respected element of the society. Programs to fight alcoholism are more respected and more supported than supporting small business on the rez." A Manderson businessman argues that the perception of Lakota business people as well off does not take into account their family obligations: "I mean like people might say that [business people] have a lot of money, but that money is for bread on the table and for their families. They should realize that small business people are relatives too and have to act like relatives."

Despite their cultural ties to the communities they serve, Lakota-owned small businesses are subject to shoplifting, bad debt, and vandalism. A Wanbli businesswoman complains, "People just don't care that they are hurting your business." Most of the crime is attributed to Lakota youth. A Pine Ridge business popular with young people has never had a break-in. The owner accounts for his good fortune by reasoning that "the kids protect it themselves." The owner of a Rosebud business describes being burglarized by Lakota boys and the consequences: "Three boys broke into our offices, and the police caught them in the act. I figured out the damages and told the boys that they could work off the damages at five dollars an hour, totaling three hundred dollars. Two of them agreed, and they worked all summer doing windows, cleaning up, mowing, whatever came up. The third one said he didn't want to work, and his grandmother said she was going to send him back down to Texas with his folks because he wouldn't do anything she asked."

Lakotas' emphasis on egalitarianism and redistribution also depresses the prices Lakota small businesses can charge. For Lakota professionals, it is often difficult to charge customers what their training and experience merit. One St. Francis businessman struggles with this problem:

My time is worth fifty dollars an hour. A lot don't want to pay that, they want to pay five dollars, but my service is worth a lot more than that. It was a hard thing for me, I just had to do a contract rather than talking money over the phone or wrangling with the person. I just say, "I'll send my contract to you and if it's agreeable with you, fine," because it's hard to say fifty dollars. They say, "Gee, that's a lot of money," and then right away the price starts coming down, "Well, how about forty dollars," and next thing you know, it's not worth it. So like I had to teach myself to be assertive. Then you got to have that confidence that, yes, I am worth fifty or sixty dollars an hour. If you do a good job and they're happy with it, then that helps build your confidence up even more for next time. But it took me a long time to get to a point to say this is what I need to get this job done. I think a lot of people around here are having that same mindset, about what they're worth. Another guy, he does everything, woodcutting, painting, yardwork, but he asks for a price, and then he says, "What can you pay?" and they'll say ten dollars, so he ends up working five hours for ten dollars. If you're putting in five hours of work, you're not even getting minimum wage.

A concession many Lakota enterprises make to Lakota values is "Indian pricing." Within the Lakota community, it was common for small business producers to have different sets of prices, consisting of a sliding scale for Lakotas and a higher fixed price for non-Indians. For Lakota customers, small businesses often make price adjustments depending on the financial circumstances of the customer. A local mechanic shop owner in Rosebud told me about his sliding scale of charges: "I have two different pricing scales. If folks can't afford it, at least I get the cost of parts out of it. If people have jobs, I charge eighteen dollars an hour. If they're elderly, or they don't have a job or have lots of kids, I charge what the parts cost, or what they can afford." Social pressure discourages Lakota service enterprises from imposing a markup for keeping manufactured goods on hand. An Antelope repairman admits: "I leave the prices on the things I bought, and that's what I charge my customers."

Indian pricing is only partially explainable by the market analysis of determining the price at which supply and demand meet. There are also emotional and cultural attachments to the community that make the contradictions between profit motives and generosity toward extended kin unbearable for some. As a woman from Rosebud explains: "It's harder with us [Lakota business people] if you have some traditional values. Like me, I gave them picture frames I made away, and I think for a lot of us like me initially, I think it's why the concept of business hasn't gone over so well among Indians is the value system is different." Some mention motivations other than cash returns for starting their small businesses, such as creating social credit, keeping the peace, and supporting community values. An owner of a Rosebud car repair business concurs with the last-mentioned motivation: "I don't worry about making it big. To me, people are the key. It's better to scrape by and help people out along the way. I'm here for the people." Helping the community affects how a Rosebud seamstress conducts business: "I sewed two sun dance dresses, have to have them done by Thursday. The woman can't pay until the 31st, but I made them for her, to encourage her. Sometimes people ask me to sew when they can't afford it, but I help them out. And I sew for local charities. So everything isn't just sewing to make money off it."

Another Lakota value pervasive in Lakota small business is the importance of family. A common aspiration of Lakota small business producers is to run a family business. Most Lakota small business people I spoke with prefer to work with family members and made an effort to recruit members of their immediate and extended families. Indeed, most Lakota businesses involve family. One small mechanic business in Wanbli is owned and operated by two brothers. "I don't do much out here now," one brother remarks, "but I built this business up myself. My brother used to do mechanics in Mission, and that's how he came to be known, so he came out here and technically he's bought me out, but I ain't seen any of the money yet. For everyone's purposes, I'm not doing nothing anymore, but I help him out." Another brother who works for BIA maintenance was on vacation for a month, so he was repairing his own car and helping his brothers out. One of the mechanic's sons did the bookkeeping for the business. Family working arrangements in small businesses are usually structured to benefit all parties. For example, one Mission businesswoman who owns a building provides an apartment in the building for her brother so he, in turn, can supply security for the building at night and have a place to live.

One reason family members are recruited to a small business is that relatives are trustworthy. Some Lakotas say that family members are the only people they trust in a business arrangement. A Wanbli woman expresses a typical distrust of going into business with nonrelatives: "What they really need here is a cigarette smoke shop, because now people mostly go to Rapid to buy their smokes, and it costs a lot of money to do that. I was going to go in with some people to set one up, but then I pulled out because I decided I didn't trust anybody. A lot of Indian people don't trust." A man from Manderson agrees: "I guess working together really parallels the family idea, that it's easier to meet and organize when you work together, and you can trust your relatives and eventually maybe people you work with, but it's a lot harder with strangers." A man from

Kyle attributes part of the problem of trust to the political history of the reservation: "I think the people around here really had their trust abused, with the BIA, the [tribal] council, so you need to go down to the grass roots with the original traditional way people would organize, around their families, take that part of the old along with the new and go with it."

Even the most successful Lakota business people take into account their family and religious obligations when making business decisions. A businessman from the Rosebud Reservation recalls: "I closed my first business in 1986, with the recession, plus my grandfather died, then my dad, and my brother had surgery, so I had to meet my family's needs at that time." A St. Francis businesswoman left the management of her convenience store to her employees while she attended a sun dance for four days. A businesswoman from Porcupine buys her supplies from a more distant source because the seller is a relative. These social considerations extend to close family friends as well. An Antelope entrepreneur observes: "I exchanged my inventory for debt repayment, but they still haven't paid it off. I probably would have done something by now, except that they are such close friends with my wife that she wouldn't let me anyway."

Lakota small business people also help their communities by providing needed wage labor jobs. Although none of the small businesses is large enough to support a hundred employees, several hire more than a dozen workers, and virtually all of them have at least one full-time worker who is not an immediate family member. Convenience and retail stores employ young people for minimum wage as baggers and shelf stockers. Gas stations and private mechanic shops hire mechanics and clerks to help with the workload. A small mechanic shop owner from Rosebud reports: "I have two employees, one that works hourly wages, and the other works on commission. The young guy, he gets six dollars an hour. I have to work two days a week just to pay him sometimes. I really can't afford employees, but it's too much work for me to do alone."

Small business people see themselves as role models for the next generation of Lakotas. People who are currently engaged in small business are self-conscious about the example they are setting for their children and community. "I think trying out small business has affected my household positively," a woman from Antelope told me. "It's provided an example to my kids of the kinds of things they can do, and it's something available for them to do too."

Market-based forms of production are limited on the Pine Ridge and Rosebud Reservations. The peripheral position of these reservations within the U.S. economy means that wage work is difficult to find and that the hours, pay, and conditions of wage work are often less than desired. For those few Lakotas who engage in small business, capital and customers are scarce, and they frequently face stiff competition from other Lakotas and from well-funded multinational corporations.

Lakota culture affects the structure and practice of these market-based forms of production. As we have seen, the Lakotas' experiences and interpretations of wage work are guided by Lakota values of kinship, nonmaterialism, and belief in an abundance of support available through local social relations. Small business people are challenged to pursue their profit motive within the cultural context of sharing, generosity, and responsibility toward those in need. Although these cultural values may initially appear to have a negative impact on the Lakotas' commitment to and success from market-based economic activities, the reality of the limited returns available within the economic periphery makes such cultural values an essential safeguard for those times when elusive market opportunities shrink even further.

3

Alternative Economic Activities

In economic peripheries such as Pine Ridge and Rosebud, there is no dependable access to mainstream market-based forms of making a living. As a result, most Lakotas engage in alternatives to wage labor or formal small business. Although these alternatives might appear to be outside the normal channels of the market economy, they too are affected by the world economy.

On the reservations, there are a large number of informal, single-person microenterprise operations with no capitalization, inventory, or overhead. Microenterprise represents the smallest yet most widespread form of Lakota economic activity. It is estimated that 83 percent of households in Pine Ridge engage in some form of microenterprise, with 5 percent of households having no other source of cash income (Sherman 1988). The average annual income of microenterprise households in Pine Ridge participating in a peer group lending program in 1992 was $14,720, with $2,120 net business income; although the amount of income made through microenterprise is not large, it is enough to raise 21 percent of these microenterprise households above the poverty line (Mushinski and Pickering 1996:159–61). The Lakotas involved in microenterprises generally have less formal education and training than those involved in small businesses: 20 percent of them never went beyond the eighth grade, and another 17 percent ended their education before completing high school and had GED equivalency diplomas (Mushinski and Pickering 1996:153).

Microenterprises focus on production of traditional Lakota goods such as beadwork, star quilts, and Indian dancing outfits, and nontraditional goods and services such as work clothes, food and catering, car repair and cleaning, hair cutting, and babysitting. Most operate out of the home. With no obvious business location or commercial appearance, they must be found by word of mouth. Most Lakota microenterprises market their goods by selling door to door. Other common markets include local or regional events such as powwows or Indian art shows.

Lakota microenterprises follow an annual cycle of high production during the winter and lower production in the summer. A Wanbli beader comments on this cyclical pattern: "In the winter I make things to have on hand, so I have stuff to sell people who come through in the summer like from California and all." Microenterprise production peaks during the winter months because it is difficult to travel, fewer temporary wage jobs are available, and there are fewer local activities to attend. As one Kyle quilter puts it, "I get a lot done in the winter, since there is no place to go."

Such microenterprises have operated on the reservations for decades. There are references to the casual sales of native crafts for cash in a 1930 economic census of the Pine Ridge Reservation (FARC Pine Ridge, Item 151, Boxes 905–907; Macgregor 1946:48). A Rosebud woman recalls: "Star quilts were popular by the '30s and '40s. My mom made some to sell and some to give away." Others were not sure whether their parents or grandparents gave away, exchanged, or sold what they made at home.

Another realm of Lakota activities generates income, goods, and services, but these activities are sporadic, irregular, and uncertain. Odd jobs such as hauling things away or cleaning up may last only a few hours. Local, regional, and national competitions in powwow dancing, rodeo, and sports such as softball and volleyball infrequently result in a hoped-for prize for some Lakotas. Large regional and national powwows provide an opportunity for the best Indian dancers to compete for thousands of dollars over a three- or four-day period. Local powwows are often combined with giveaways and feeds, which supply gifts, household items, and food to members of the community. Rodeo competition is as close to a professional sport as can be found on the reservations. As early as the 1930s, Lakotas traveled to compete in rodeos for cash prizes (Mekeel 1936:78).

Subsistence activities continue to play a role in the reservation economy, although most Lakota households are not living or producing on land they own. Even those Lakotas who have retained title to their allotted land often lease that land to non-Indians for agricultural commodity production. Family gardens that supplement purchased foodstuffs continue to exist but are not prevalent. Wild plants remain an important component of the distinctive diet of reservation residents. Lakotas gather wild turnips (*thípsila*), chokecherries, wild plums, buffaloberries, and Indian tea; eat them fresh or dry them; and use them for traditional foods such as soup and pudding (*wóȟapi*). The Great Plains has a five- to eight-year climatic cycle, ranging from lush, cool, green summers with floods to dry, hot, barren summers with droughts. The availability of wild plants turns on the date of the last frost and the amount of moisture in the spring and summer.

Many Lakotas still hunt and fish. Since the beginning of the reservations, the range and abundance of game within their boundaries has not been adequate to supply the Lakotas. Nevertheless, the majority of Lakota households, such as those on Pine Ridge, rely on some form of hunting, fishing, and gathering for subsistence (Sherman 1988).

The Household Mix

Households embody a mix of market and nonmarket activities. The character and extent of production in the household turns in large part on the composition of its members at a given time. The diversity of and changes in household members mean that most Lakota households have access to a range of economic resources. For example, in one extended family household of ten working-age adults, three elders, and eleven children, seven are engaged in full-time wage work, one cares for the elderly and the children at home, and one is unemployed but looking into college courses. Another household includes a quilter, a disability-benefits recipient, a seasonal wage laborer who drives a school bus, and a full-time student who helps make and sell the quilts. A third household consists of an elderly disabled man who receives a civil service pension; his wife, who provides him with home health care and has a sewing microenterprise; and their grandchildren, who are students.

Some family members contribute their wages, work-related benefits, land-lease checks, or access to public benefits to the household. Others contribute domestic labor such as food production, sewing, babysitting, and house cleaning. College students can often qualify for monthly federal Pell Grant stipends. One member of a household might focus on meeting the ceremonial and social obligations of the family, and others might gather wild plants, hunt, or garden.

For Lakota households with small children or elders needing care, a family member who cares for them allows others to engage in wage labor or other market-based economic activities outside the home. Caretakers may also engage in some form of microenterprise at home such as additional babysitting or beadwork. "I have to watch some of my grandkids, so I sew quilts at the table," a Kyle woman reports. "It means I can't sew steady. I exchange with my daughter for her help around the house, and she helps out with bills." Another Rosebud quilter has thirteen grandchildren, so she both quilts and babysits.

Even children contribute to the household economic mix, as a Rosebud woman describes: "The older ones really help by watching out for the little ones. My oldest daughter is going to be fourteen, so I said if she stayed home with the kids I would pay her, and it really helps me out. She helps with the house chores and she watches the kids. And then whatever I pay her, she can buy what she wants with that. I pay my oldest boy for taking out trash and doing yardwork. It's a way for them to make extra money while they have to stay home. And like at school or summer programs, he's always coming up with odd jobs to do for money."

A family member receiving some form of public assistance or work-related benefits can often supplement or meet the cash needs of a household engaged in nonmarket forms of production. Those Lakotas who are not currently working sometimes receive forms of financial support as a result of their prior years of wage labor: retirement pensions, Social Security retirement and disability benefits, workman's compensation claims, or unemployment insurance. In 1990, 34 percent of the households in Pine Ridge and 33 percent in Rosebud were receiving work-related benefits. The mean Social Security annual benefit that year was $4,000, and the mean retirement benefit amount was $4,500.

Lakota Household Production: A Fall-Back Position

Household production is time-consuming and provides limited returns for Lakotas, yet it is often viewed as ideal or necessary when vital goods or services are too expensive or not available locally or when one is out of a job and has plenty of time. By maintaining various forms of household production for direct consumption, barter, and cash exchange, Lakotas can fill the often significant gaps left by the broader market-based economy in ways that confirm Lakota preferences, values, and styles. It is often possible for Lakotas to fall back on household microenterprise production because it requires only a small capital investment. All that a bead-worker needs, for example, is leather, beads, thread, and needles.

Microenterprises in Lakota households can help compensate for reservation unemployment and underemployment. For example, household members sometimes pursue subsistence activities for direct consumption or exchange. As mentioned previously, Lakotas hunt and gather porcupine, deer meat, wild turnips, chokecherries, and other wild plants. These are consumed directly or sold to traditional artisans, to food producers, and to others for their ceremonial and dietary needs. Hunting and gathering take considerably more time than grocery shopping, but no cash is required to obtain their products.

As discussed in the previous chapter, operating microenterprises out of Lakota households can provide a crucial supplement to insufficient wages brought in by seasonal, temporary, or part-time work. Among thirty microenterprise producers from Rosebud and Pine Ridge with whom I spoke, 65 percent were unemployed. Those Lakotas with no wage jobs juggle several forms of self-employment.

Many Lakota extended families rely on household production to supplement their income. A Kyle woman began beading and sewing full time when her children were little and she could not work outside the home, but she returned to being a full-time language instructor when her children were older. A medicine man from Kyle supplements a pension by making traditional crafts. A Manderson woman works full time but also sews to make extra money for her family.

Lakota household production activities slide into different markets with ease. In practice, there are no firm lines between Lakota household production for direct use, informal microenterprise production, and formal microenterprise activities. One form of household production blends into the others. A Lakota woman may begin making ribbon shirts for her immediate family, start receiving requests from neighbors and friends to make shirts for sale, and develop her craft into a cottage industry with a business license, using family members and friends to assist in production for sale in local stores. When the fad is over, she returns to sewing only for family members. Local mechanics start out fixing their own cars and may end up running a repair shop for the entire community. In discussing his Rosebud car repair business, one man explains: "At first I was just doing it for friends and stuff, and then grew into more of a regular thing." An Antelope seamstress recalls the gradual way she expanded and formalized her microenterprise: "I always did kind of watch my mother sew, and that helped me, you know, to sew better. I don't remember my mom setting down and making us sit down and watch her sew. You more or less automatically watched her and you learned from watching her. Like all my sisters learned how to sew, and we learned to cook and bake. I always did kind of sew, mostly for myself and my husband, I made him shirts, and then for my sons I made them shirts, you know. Then as time went on I got into sewing for other people, and more or less built up my business."

Supplies for household enterprises are informally and infrequently obtained. They are most often purchased on trips to border towns or regional cities to buy other goods. An Antelope plumber explains: "I get my supplies in Winner and Valentine, when my family needs to go to town for supplies anyway." The price of supplies, such as fabric, food, parts, or cosmetic goods, is highest at local reservation shops. Cloth, for example, is two to four dollars more per yard in the local reservation shops than in regional cities such as Rapid City or Sioux Falls. Those Lakotas with more capital have the capacity to travel to cities where the prices of supplies are the lowest, and they are often able to make bulk purchases there. Those with more limited resources must buy their materials at overpriced local reservation shops and consequently make smaller profits from their sales.

Not surprisingly, in these communities situated on the edge of the cash economy, Lakotas commonly use noncash transactions such as barter, trade, and rummage to obtain supplies for their household microenterprises. As a Porcupine woman explains: "I'm making a star quilt for a guy in the Czech Republic. When he gets my quilt, he's going to send me beads to sell." Secondhand goods are a source of affordable, though unpredictable, local supplies. A beader from Wanbli uses old leather jackets given to her or obtained from rummage. Some supplies for an Oglala seamstress also came from rummage: "You know one time my daughter was working at the office, and she called and said that some people have sent some rummage from New York, and she got into it and there was a big plastic bag full of thread, so she just grabbed that for me and it was about thirty spools. It was all odd colors, pretty colors too. That really helped me out a lot, because when I need one special thread for a particular color, I use that. This iron I bought for five dollars at rummage, but it's a good one."

Barter or exchange-in-kind is regularly mentioned as the most lucrative form of exchange for Lakota microenterprise producers. The overall shortage of cash income prevents most reservation residents from paying high prices for anything, including traditional Lakota items. It is possible, however, for a skilled quilter to exchange a star blanket worth $450 for a set of beaded cuffs and armbands also worth $450. Both parties feel they receive the benefit of the bargain since each invests only about $80 worth of materials and neither pays cash for the skilled labor of the other.

Even household producers cannot completely avoid market-regulated transactions, such as the purchase of materials. The effects of cash transactions, however, can be somewhat mitigated by extending Lakota-form social relations to the marketplace. For example, several beadworkers ceremonially adopted non-Indians from the East Coast or California who were involved in the sales of beads and other essential beadworking materials. The beadworkers were then able to obtain the lowest wholesale prices for those materials from their new relatives. A quill worker developed the relationship of sister to a Navajo man when they participated in Native American Church ceremonies together. Because of their relationship, he provided her with a tanned hide from Montana each year.

Similarly, when Lakota household producers make sales of traditional items to stores, most expect a relationship of personal respect to develop. Beadworkers may terminate profitable relationships with regional stores because the store's buyer haggles about price or comments on the quality of the item and thus loses the respect of the beadworker. One quilter from Rosebud recalls: "That guy at the [local craft store], he said my quilts weren't good and ran down my designs, just to get me to lower my prices, so I don't go there anymore. And the guy at the [local tourist shop], he hardly buys anything, he's really choosy about the styles and colors, and I hear he only buys a lot from his relatives."

Whether to supplement low wages, a lost job, or inadequate public assistance payments, household production provides a way for many Lakotas to meet family needs. The low costs associated with starting household production together with social and cultural methods of obtaining supplies and outlets makes household production an important and readily available form of economic activity on the reservation.

Family Support and Self-Sufficiency

Lakota households strive to be as self-sufficient as possible. Family members are sometimes forced to learn how to repair appliances, cars, electrical wiring, or plumbing themselves because no one is available in the community to hire. A local Lakota plumber may be affordable because of Indian pricing, but the demand for his services often means one must wait a few days before a sink can be unclogged. Border town plumbers are expensive, charging not only a premium hourly rate but also the mileage to drive forty miles or more to come onto the reservation. Similarly, one local car repair shop had such a backlog of repairs that some cars had been in the shop for five months. The possibility of such tremendous delays motivates Lakotas to learn how to repair their own vehicles.

Family ties free many Lakotas from hiring contractors on the open market. Lakotas with useful skills are called on to provide their services to extended family members outside their households. A brother-in-law who works as a plumber might be asked to offer advice and ultimately labor to put in a new bathroom or renovate an old house. Even relatives visiting for a short time might lend a hand with household projects for their relatives: installing appliances, building on rooms, or repairing cars. There are innumerable stories of women making dresses for their sisters, daughters, nieces, or granddaughters for special occasions such as graduation, special presentations, or dances.

Many Lakotas aspire to begin a family business made up of the productive activities of multiple members of a household. In such cases, the Lakotas' emphasis on the extended family has a direct structural effect on the composition of a business. One Rosebud woman confesses, "I was hoping to have a business with my family, because my daughter quilts, and my sister-in-law across the way does, and my son he can make cabinets and things out of wood, so we could all work together." A beadworker from Parmelee, whose husband was a painter, sees that her daughter is getting interested in quill and beads, and her mother beads and quilts, so she hopes they can have a family business. A Kyle man has several children who quill, bead, and paint, and he wants to set up a family arts and crafts shop.

Expressions of Lakota Culture

Lakotas are also motivated to take up household production because they see it as expressing their cultural identity. Hunting and gathering, for example, are still practiced and still regarded as quintessential aspects of Lakota culture. A wide range of Lakotas working at a variety of occupations hunt and gather because it is a Lakota thing to do. An attorney from Rosebud hunts every year to provide meat for his mother's annual community feed. A woman from Pine Ridge with a college degree alternates between working away from the reservation and engaging in horticulture, hunting, gathering, and microenterprise on the reservation. A woman with a master's degree is also experienced in Lakota methods for butchering wild game, a skill she learned from her mother.

Beadworkers and producers of other traditional items are proud of their work and feel their crafts are maintaining a distinctive Lakota tradition, albeit with some changes. Traditional items are still considered Lakota, but many producers acknowledge changes over the last twenty years. According to an Antelope woman: "They're getting back into more of the traditional things to do, like you see a lot more beadwork than you used to, and you see a lot of different ways to do beadwork. And you see a lot more star quilts. More people are involved in making things to make ends meet now. In the past, people made things, but they made it and gave it away. Now they're making it for an income."

The most traditional form of production on the reservations is in fact Lakota items produced within the home. Unlike small business people, who must conform to mainstream ideals of training and operations, household producers embody the type of training and expertise that is born of following Lakota traditions. Relatives with special skills in creating traditional items teach their nephews and nieces their skills, "to help them be able to make money." Although books and courses on making beadwork are available, 28 of the 30 Lakota beadworkers with whom I spoke learned how to bead from a relative, and all 30 were teaching younger relatives how to bead. Children watch relatives making beaded items; those who express an interest in learning beadwork themselves are given a small amount of leather and beads by a relative and told to take the materials and come back with a finished item. When it is completed, the child is given additional materials to make a slightly larger item. Once the young beadworker becomes a competent beader, he or she in turn encourages younger relatives to learn beading by giving them materials for practice. A Potato Creek porcupine quill worker learned her craft through this custom: "My aunt taught me quill work by giving me small amounts of quills." A beadworker from Wanbli told me: "When my nieces visit, I have them do beadwork for me and then I pay them for it, so they learn to use their hands too."

Other types of traditional Lakota skills are transmitted and learned through a similar intergenerational process. A Kyle woman comments: "I learned when I was young watching my mom sew, bead, and quilt. I've been making things for sale for twenty years now." A Rosebud quilter is teaching her granddaughter the craft. The quilter sews the star blocks together, and "then I give it to my granddaughter to quilt. I'm just now teaching her to cut out the squares. Pretty soon she'll be sewing them up too."

Lakotas regard the practice and process of creating traditional items, and not just the objects themselves, as bound up with distinctly Lakota values. Household producers thus become examples of Lakota culture for their children and community. As a Wanbli woman makes apparent, at least some are consciously attempting to revive the Lakota values of industry and hard work within a family setting:

> I used to party a lot, it was really controlling my life, but I don't have time for that now, and my beading helped me make that change and get to where I am today. I used to be bored, that alcohol seemed like the only way to get some excitement into the day. But now I've changed, spiritually and emotionally too. So I'm encouraging others, to help them realize that there are things to do every day, that there is no excuse for sitting around bored and drinking. With your hands, you could do anything you put your mind to, you shouldn't just leave them sitting still. Now my niece is trying to bead since she said she was bored. I don't let anybody walk in my house but I'm sitting them down with needles and a plate of beads to keep their hands busy. I don't see any sense in just sitting in front of the TV, you might as well be making something.

Household production, on one level an economic activity, also sustains family ties and some cultural traditions for the Lakotas. However, the domestic realm of production is not insulated from the effects of economic incorporation. The world economy intrudes, sometimes subtly, even into activities and places that Lakotas call their own.

Pricing

The effects of the world economy increase as a Lakota household expands from production for direct consumption and gifts to microenterprise production for sale. At the same time, this process is tempered by local cultural conventions that work to keep market forces from entirely shaping and defining the transactions surrounding household production.

Pricing handmade items is an important arena of contestation between Lakota culture and the world economy. Lakotas consider a number of factors when pricing items made in their homes. The price of perceived comparable items in off-reservation stores is often used as a starting point. Unfortunately, equating the prices of handmade items with manufactured items undervalues the labor of Lakota household producers. For example, a Rosebud quilter uses children's comforters in the J. C. Penney catalog as a price base for her star blankets. Others compare their prices with those charged by local entrepreneurs: "I set my prices based on what people around here charge, or what they say other people charge."

Lakotas who make traditional items in their homes sell their items primarily to local individuals but sometimes also sell to local shops, non-Indian tourists, and regional shops. Locally, prices are depressed by the combination of an abundant supply of traditional Lakota items and the low income of potential purchasers. In local sales situations, prices are often set by an immediate cash need, not by the cost of labor and supplies.

Lakota culture also affects pricing. There is sometimes a general reluctance by Lakotas to reduce traditional items to a cash value. As one quill worker in Potato Creek points out: "Old people say [traditional quill work] is priceless." A Wanbli beader is also hesitant to assign a price to such items: "I like to make things, but I don't like selling that much. I hate to ask for money for them."

Community members also pressure local sellers of goods and services to be fair in their pricing. "I'm afraid people might say I'm too greedy," one artisan remarks, "that I really want money, so I don't raise my prices and sell them for less." One woman who sells Indian tacos at a concession stand at powwows keeps handy the containers of cheese, flour, and oil that she uses to prepare the tacos, in order to counter accusations that she charges full price but uses free food provided through the USDA Commodities Program to make the tacos.

The issue of pricing sometimes causes tensions between Lakota households that use microenterprise largely to supplement wage income and those that depend heavily on microenterprise sales. Items produced by the former households are often priced lower than those in the latter. One Potato Creek quill worker sees herself as a victim of this price discrepancy: "I don't want anybody to copy my work and change my prices, like that, and here somebody did. So it kind of ruined my business. Toward Rapid City there's one person who does that. She sells hers real cheap, so when I took mine that way, they wanted to buy it for that much, and I didn't want to sell it like that. But she didn't hardly do it that much, so it's kind of ruined that way, because when she sells it, she sells it just once in a while, because her husband is working in Pine Ridge, he's making good money. But it's ruined my price. I guess she don't know what to sell for, and she don't want to ask me because she copied my work."

The price of an item made in household production can also depend on culturally specific market practices. Like Lakota small businesses, household producers by convention acknowledge an Indian price that is substantially lower than the price non-Indians are charged. Local Indians are therefore less willing to pay full price. A Rosebud woman comments on this pricing custom: "People who do crafts have an Indian price and a price for white people. One guy called me up and said he was braiding some *thípsila* [wild turnips], and I was thinking about wanting some *thípsila* braid. So I said, 'What are you asking?' And he said, 'Well, last year I had a six-foot braid and this white lady she paid me ninety dollars for it.' I said, 'Well, this Indian lady will probably pay you fifteen dollars,' and he laughed. Because usually they will just go around to the offices and take whatever people are willing to pay around here."

Lakota household producers will often make adjustments to price depending on the financial circumstances of a native customer. A woman who makes clothing out of her home in Antelope adheres to such a pricing scheme:

> I more or less kind of try to stay within what I think people can afford. I don't have a set price. I never charged that much [for sewing]. A lot of times I'd do it just for doing something for people. If someone comes in for a dress and it looks like they don't have much, I charge what I think they can afford. Some of the Indian people are hard up, but they want a dancing dress, and you know they could probably come up with the money if you asked them for it, but it would be hard for them because in my working days [in the boarding school] I knew how they wanted things and how

hard it was for them. But then the people who are working who I know can afford it, then I charge them regular price, and try to stay in the same kind of price range for those kind of people.

A seamstress from Kyle admits: "If they barely make ends meet, I charge them half price." A beader from Potato Creek similarly believes: "I have a tender heart, and feel they can't pay because they're Indian." This pricing practice is culturally conditioned, but it has a world-market consequence. By accepting lower compensation, household producers respond to and absorb the financial straits of their friends and neighbors, who confront low wages and uncertain terms of employment.

Sales Space

The world economy also affects household production through its emphasis on sales space. Lakota household producers rarely have nondomestic outlets for their enterprise. The low population density precludes open marketplaces like those found in Latin America or Asia. The only concentration of potential buyers is found in villages with bureaucratic offices, such as Pine Ridge, Kyle, Mission, and Rosebud. Because most villages on the reservations are at least thirty miles apart, transportation costs needed to find a buyer can be significant. "On the rez," a small craft producer from Rosebud observes, "it's better to sell out of your home, rather than to have the overhead of a shop. The economy here, it's like $3,200 per person, so unless you're real big, like that craft shop that sells supplies, you can't afford it." Households subsidize the price of services and goods sold by taking space and time from their members. Running a microenterprise out of the home places a burden on the household. A Rosebud woman who fixes hair agrees: "The problem that I have is when I do hair here at home, like when I have perms or haircuts, I have to hurry up and clean, and my husband always finds someplace to go. It's bad when you have to rush home and fix supper and do dishes and clean up, because I do a lot in my kitchen, the rinses and stuff, so I have to get the dishes done and everything."

Furthermore, regulations prohibiting the use of HUD housing for business purposes create a special difficulty for small businesses and the large number of microenterprises, especially as virtually no low-cost commercial rental space is available. That in turn adds to the hidden nature of this less formal sector of the economy. It also creates pressure on household producers to sell their products at low prices to middlemen with storefronts. These middlemen are then able to sell Indian-made items eagerly sought by some in the dominant society at a substantial markup.

Working Conditions

Household production might appear to offer some freedom from the more negative conditions of wage labor. The pace and intensity of household production is controlled by the Lakota artisan or service provider and his or her household. No outsider regulates the number of hours per day or items per week that must be produced. Household control of production means that microenterprise producers are free to attend religious ceremonies, travel to regional powwows, or spend time with relatives or friends who visit from outside the reservation, particularly during the summer. More production thus occurs during the winter months when travel is difficult and there are fewer community events to attend. Many household producers feel they are their own boss, free of the rigidities and mistreatment associated with wage labor. A small-scale plumber from Antelope explains: "I like to work for myself, because I can squeeze in time to go fishing. When I have contract jobs, I always try to get them done as quickly as possible so I'll have time to fish. Others are always telling me to slow down so I'll get more money out of them, but I get new contracts after I try to work as quick as I can. I get a house done in a day or day and a half when others take a week."

Pressing economic needs or the requirements of customers, however, can increase the intensity of household production, sometimes even beyond that of a wage labor position. The experience of one Rosebud quilter illustrates this problem: "This quilting is really just like working. I get up early and work all day until midnight. Even if I take just one day off, I get behind. I finally finish an order for a break, and then it starts all over again. My family is used to me working hard. They're always telling me to take a break, but then I get behind right away and have to work even harder." As Lakota household production becomes more commodified — if, for example, a beadworker must fill orders for beadwork from regional tourist shops — the household begins to lose control over the pace of production. The beader may lose the opportunity for future orders if items cannot be made according to the tourist shop's schedule. A woman from Parmelee encounters such a situation producing at home for a regional beadwork store: "I don't know how much time I spend beading. The least amount I would say is 6 hours each day, but sometimes somebody comes up with an emergency, like they need some moccasins in two days, and then I have to put in twelve hours a day to get them done."

Some Lakotas have made attempts through cooperative organizations to manage and control household production of traditional crafts such as beadwork, quill work, and star quilts, but they have met with limited success. Cooperative organizations have been most effective managing the purchase of materials and marketing but have been less successful regulating production. For example, officials from Disneyland once expressed interest in selling beadwork with Mickey Mouse beaded into berets and other items. However, there was no centralized organization for Lakota beadworkers that could dictate the style and type of items to be produced or regulate the schedule of production for Disneyland's sales counters.

Lakota Ceremonies, Religion, and Household Production

Household production for traditional Lakota ceremonial and religious occasions represents another realm of modern Lakota life that is simultaneously shaped by cultural conventions and aspects of the world economy. Many community and religious ceremonies seem to be representative, if not archetypical, of Lakota tradition. Yet these cultural practices are affected in various ways by wage work and commodification of traditional items.

Feeds and Giveaways

Community giveaways are held for several reasons: as part of annual pow-wows, to commemorate graduations, as memorials for departed loved ones, as part of naming and *hųká,* or adoption, ceremonies, and in conjunction with other events that involve honoring an individual or group (E. Deloria 1944:77–78; Goldfrank 1943:79–81; Hassrick 1964:37; A. Kehoe 1989:65; Young Bear and Theisz 1994:58–59). These events range from local community gatherings of around fifty people to the annual reservation-wide gatherings of several thousand people. During these occasions, the sponsoring family distributes the objects it has made or purchased to the entire local or reservation community; there is no cash charge imposed on those who consume these items beyond a vague obligation of long-term generalized reciprocity (Grobsmith 1981:129–30; see J. Moore 1993:240–69). Specific objects, such as star quilts or beaded items, are presented to Lakotas who are called to come forward to be thanked or honored by the family sponsoring the giveaway. Cash gifts are often made to the drum groups and the announcer at the event. Other general items — blankets, towels, fabric, clothing, and trunks — are spread around the dance circle and are selected by groups of people called forward, such as the dancers, drummers, or elders. Certain smaller objects — kitchen utensils, plastic containers, and toys — are brought around and distributed so that every member in the audience receives something.

Often accompanying a giveaway or sponsored independently is a "feed," in which food is spread out across a line of tables and everyone is invited to bring a plate and bowl through a line to be served. Foods vary from the traditional wild turnip (*thípsila*) and deer meat soup and wild chokecherry pudding (*wóȟapi*) to contemporary processed items such as white bread, fried chicken, and sheet cake. People are encouraged to take any remaining food home in a *wathéča* bucket (*wathéča* being food one takes home from a feast). Held frequently in conjunction with give-aways and powwows are competitions such as softball and little league, rodeos, and a contest for young women to compete through local, tribal, and national events to become Miss Indian Nation.

Families sponsoring the giveaway event must amass the food, goods, and cash needed to carry off a successful occasion. Although the accumulation of giveaway goods is part of a long Lakota tradition, the world economy has many observable effects on this process, such as bank loans, store-bought goods, and cash purchases of traditional Lakota items to be given away.

Most Lakotas who spoke with me did not explicitly calculate the cost of hosting a giveaway but generally reported that it took two years to accumulate the goods to be distributed. Personal loans for several hundred or several thousand dollars are often obtained to support a family giveaway. "I had a giveaway of fifty quilts that cost me about one thousand dollars," a woman from St. Francis reports, "and made a bank loan of two thousand dollars to pay for the materials and the quilters I hired, and I gave them my TV and stereo for quilting too!" Because of the frequency of such events, and the custom of holding a memorial only one year after the death of a family member, Lakota households are constantly accumulating goods for giveaways. "I have all this stuff," a Rosebud woman explains, "but it's for a giveaway—potholders, quilts, pillows." A Pine Ridge woman has a strategy for accumulating goods: "I put money away as I get it so it's not so hard just before the giveaway. We buy things as they come up on sale, like at Alco or K-Mart, for the blankets and stuff like that. Usually we end up spending about a hundred dollars on meat each time. Lots of times we buy those Banquet frozen chicken in a box and heat those up."

Given the costs involved, not all Lakota families can sponsor give-aways. Yet the level of a family's contributions to community needs does not appear to correlate directly with their income level. "Here people give away as a sign of wealth," a woman from Antelope told me, "because I know people who don't have food in the cupboard but a year after the death, they have a giveaway." Some Lakota households with the fewest apparent resources have the greatest reputations for generosity, calling on the aid of a wider, closer group of family members to compensate for smaller amounts of individual income.

There is a trade-off between devoting more time and family members to making giveaway items and spending more money to buy items to give away. Some families make the objects for giveaways themselves. This includes the household of a woman from Rosebud: "I started making quilts when I was putting up a dinner for my sister who passed away, so I needed quilts for that." Sometimes traditional items that are part of a giveaway are purchased from microenterprise producers.

The physical labor needed to prepare the food for a feed at a giveaway is typically provided by extended family members and friends. For noon meals, people often get up as early as three in the morning to boil potatoes, make soup, and roll fry bread. At a meal provided during an Antelope community powwow, a family served twelve turkeys, four vats of macaroni salad, four vats of potato salad, a dozen loaves of bread, three large crates full of fry bread, a dozen pies, five sheet cakes, and a trough of soup.

According to many Lakotas, the nature of giveaways and powwows has changed in recent years (Young Bear and Theisz 1994:58). "I think now people are buying and selling more beadwork," a woman from Kyle explains. "Like now at powwows, at giveaways, you really don't see a lot of beadwork given away anymore. They used to give away all kind of beadwork, but now you go to giveaways it seems like everything is store-bought, not really handmade anymore." Another woman from Kyle agreed that fewer Lakotas are producing traditional items at home for ceremonial events: "I do different beadwork like for friends of mine, like beading the eagle feather, and they say, 'Gee, we don't have the patience for that.' But I think, gee, it only takes a few hours, maybe a day or something at the longest, and they say they have no patience for it, it's so different. They're not really into the old traditional ways or anything, beadwork or anything." As a result, Lakotas more frequently use cash to purchase those traditional items that are necessary for ceremonial purposes. A woman from Rosebud points to a major reason for this change: "I learned to quilt from my mom when I was fourteen [1956]. She used to quilt all the time, and she'd make quilts for other people as favors. In those days, people made their own quilts for giveaways, and they weren't all the star quilts but whatever they knew how to make. Now the young people don't know how to do it, so they have to buy the things for the giveaway, so I'm always doing a lot of those."

Lakota Religion and Commodification

Lakota culture confronts the world economy even in the realm of religion. Cash is becoming more and more involved in the production and exchange of traditional Lakota items, the rewards for outstanding Indian dancing and singing, and even certain aspects of Lakota religious practices. Much of this commodification is revealed in an incident told by an elder from St. Francis:

> There is this small tribe in Minnesota that they call themselves the Lower Sioux. Somehow they got stuck over on that side, and they really assimilated with the whites so they have a lot of blue eyes and blond hair. But they have one of the first mega casinos, and they are really rich. And they lost most of their culture over the years, so now they're trying to learn it back. I was visiting Pipestone once and hear they were having a powwow up there, so we went, and there were people there from all over, Minneapolis, Sisseton, and beyond. They asked me if I could pray in Lakota and I said yes, and I asked if they wanted it in English too, but they said no, they didn't want no English. And they paid me for that. They paid all the dancers and the drum groups. That's what's happening now. People don't dance just for the entertainment, they just go to the powwows with the big payouts and the competition is really stiff.

Lakota religion, a source of attitudes against materialism, is also an arena of potential economic opportunity. Conflicts surrounding the authenticity of Lakota religious practices on the one hand and the tremendous interest by New Age non-Indians in Lakota religion on the other are generating serious community debates about the survival of Lakota religion (Bucko 1998:230–31). As a rule, Lakota religious leaders such as medicine men and Native American Church roadmen do not receive cash payments from those attending or benefiting from their services. However, as more non-Lakotas outside the community seek spiritual guidance and ceremonial instruction, there is growing concern over the "selling" of ceremonies to meet the lucrative curiosities of non-Indians about Lakota religion and spirituality. The ethics of accepting cash for these services, sometimes in large sums, is a point of contention in Lakota communities, as an elderly man from Manderson discusses:

> Seems like the whites wanna be Indians and the Indians wanna be whites, we're just going to end up a "wanna-be" nation. They're all going in a circle, like sheep, because spiritual-wise they're lost. I run a sun dance, and I never ask for money, and I never reject anyone. If someone does give money, then I pray about it but I take the money, because if you don't take it, they'll think you're above them or something. My brother-in-law

helps me out with the ceremonies, and he was telling me, "We're the most unlucky people I know. The other medicine men they make just lots of money, but all our white friends are poor like us!" But it all comes down to the basic Lakota beliefs, that you should pray, be honest, don't lie or steal, the things that Lakota people used to have.

As Lakota religion grows in its appeal to outsiders, it continues to become more commodified. Some tourist shops sell traditional religious items such as sage and tobacco ties, a practice that rips these objects out of their original cultural context of use. "Each of those little tobacco bundles is supposed to be your prayer," a man from Kyle wonders, "so why in the world would you buy somebody else's prayers?"

Household production and microenterprise are significant and popular alternatives to the market-based forms of economic activity taking place on the Pine Ridge and Rosebud Reservations. Lakota households are the scenes of subsistence hunting and gathering, crafts production, sewing, repairs, the production of traditional items, and other forms of goods and services that are outside the dominant society's norm of wage work.

Household production has the added benefit of allowing for the expression of Lakota culture and values within the economic arena. Rather than the individualized labor at the heart of the world economy, the household is a collective, integral economic unit, producing together, consuming together, and transmitting necessary skills and labor from one generation to the next.

The forces of the world economy nonetheless play a role even in household production. Through pricing, sales space, and the pace and intensity of the production process, household microenterprises are continually pressed to sacrifice more of their cultural space for greater economic returns. Even in the special realm of community and religious ceremonies, the ubiquity of market-based transactions continually challenges Lakotas to define and redefine their values and practices within new contexts of commodities and cash sales.

4
The Household and Consumption

Regardless of the choices Lakota households make, some external market consumption cannot be avoided. Cash is necessary for those goods and services that are not available through Lakota exchange networks or subsistence activities. Groceries, utilities, gasoline, and household goods from retail stores all require cash. The amount of money available for Lakotas to spend is minimal compared with the broader U.S. economy, however. The median annual income for households in 1990 was $10,513 in Pine Ridge and $10,211 in Rosebud, below the national poverty threshold for a family of four at that time.

The Lakotas' access to consumer goods is more constrained than their desire to consume, a tension well illustrated by a distinct monthly cycle of cash-based consumption on the reservation. Even if you forget your calendar, you can always tell when it is the beginning of the month. In the main commercial towns of Mission and Pine Ridge, through which only a handful of cars usually pass daily, every parking place is taken and cars are parked down the middle of the street. The two or three people typically in line at the post office suddenly swell to a dozen or more patrons asking for their benefit checks, buying money orders to pay bills, and sending money off to family members. Utility offices that are normally empty but for employees are filled to capacity with customers paying their bills and requesting service installations. The main grocery stores on the reservations at the beginning of the month need check-out clerks in every lane to keep up with lines of carts filled with food. Open parking lots and vacant fields are transformed into new outdoor shopping opportunities as trucks and cars haul in furniture, appliances, clothing, and toys to sell to the largest consumer crowd to be in town for the rest of the month. The roads that lead from the reservations to the main border towns for shopping also experience uncharacteristic traffic, and the grocery stores, discount stores, and restaurants in the border towns are filled with Lakotas. This flurry of activity is driven by the monthly issuance of paychecks, public assistance checks, and Social Security checks.

When this influx of money is gone, Lakota households produce items for sale to fill the gaps in cash for the rest of the month. As a result, micro-enterprise goods and services flourish toward the end of each month. In the days just before government wage, pension, and public assistance checks are received, sales of beadwork, Indian tacos, or yardwork labor become prevalent to cover shortfalls in household resources. Unfortunately, because these sales coincide with the end of the pay period for most potential customers, the prices received are far below what the labor and materials would normally demand.

Temporary Assistance to Needy Families (TANF), Supplemental Security Income (SSI), and Food Stamps introduce further complications into this monthly cycle. TANF and SSI, intended to provide the bulk of a household's nonfood needs, come out on the first of the month, whereas Food Stamps, intended to pay for food, arrive five days later. Since traveling to town to shop is an expense in itself, making two trips to shop in the space of a week is impractical. Yet money is so sparse by the end of the month that there are no reserves of food to tide the household over an additional four or five days. As a result, Lakotas inevitably use their welfare checks to buy needed food and then are faced with trying to trade Food Stamps for cash or other nonfood items that they need but have no cash benefits left to buy.

Cash-based consumption of the necessities of daily life for Lakota families has been gradually increasing over the last hundred years since the creation of the reservations. Lakota households "have been accustomed to money for a long time," maneuvering through border towns, banks, and bureaucracies to provide for household needs (Wax, Wax & Dumont 1964:20; Diamant 1988:16–17). During the earliest days of reservation life, Lakotas purchased groceries with cash raised by selling log posts, furs, wild fruits, and other products of hunting and gathering in white border towns and settlements (Cash & Hoover 1971:70, 78–79; Paine 1935:63).

Lakotas feel that they need more money to survive today than during their parents' generation. Some of this increasing dependence on cash is driven by growing desires for consumer goods and household conveniences. Elders recall as children that their family would come into town only once a month to pick up a few groceries and other essentials. After World War I, cars began to appear more regularly in Pine Ridge and Rosebud; by 1930, radios and other consumer goods were increasingly common (1930 U.S. Census). Today more and more Lakotas use cable TV and cellular phones, ameliorating the challenges of living in an extremely isolated rural area.

Cash consumption for late-twentieth-century Lakotas increasingly includes recreational activities. People travel to border towns and regional cities not just to get necessities but also for entertainment and socializing. These trips may combine shopping for essential items with window shopping, eating at a restaurant, or going to the movies; such forms of entertainment are currently absent from the reservations. "What's really going on here," a Rosebud businessman observes, "is the employees want to be able to go to Valentine or Pierre so they can do their shopping and sit and eat and have coffee while they wait for their [car] repairs, and we don't have any of that out here."

The Lakotas' need for cash is also escalated by the demands of the modern workforce. As more new jobs require higher education or vocational certification, money is needed to pay for college tuition. Lakotas work more hours or borrow more money to get training to compete for jobs. The situation of a Rosebud woman who went for vocational training and who works full-time as a secretary and at home in a microenterprise is typical: "I had a student loan that I was paying back, so I used to try to schedule enough hair appointments to make the payment on the student loan."

The general increase in cash consumption by Lakotas is not due exclusively to internal factors. Government policies have consistently fostered cash-based production and consumption to the detriment of subsistence production. Land was targeted early on by the government, which discouraged or curtailed hunting on and off the reservation. In earlier years, the BIA had little appreciation for the use of reservation lands for hunting and gathering. In a 1917 BIA assessment of allotted lands in Rosebud, the 411,843 acres used for cultivation or grazing were the only acres accounted for as in productive use. The remaining 1,132,695 acres were designated "Lands not used for any purpose" by the report, despite their wild plants and game (FARC Rosebud A-436, 8/23/17:25).

Government sales of "surplus" tribal lands to white settlers during the process of creating the Pine Ridge and Rosebud Reservations also set in motion an increasing need for money. The shrinking tribal land base, heirship fractionation, and skewed government attitudes and policies toward land use have removed land, one of the key tribal economic resources, from the hands of most Lakota households and communities.

The housing types and patterns constructed by the federal government, beginning in the 1950s and 1960s, have also contributed to the Lakotas' dependence on money. Government-built homes were not designed or constructed with a concern for minimizing the cash needed to occupy or maintain them. Home heating oil, propane, and electricity are a drain on modern Lakotas' household expenses. Cluster housing units built by HUD eliminate land between units, thus removing the opportunity for gardening. Not surprisingly, home gardening has declined significantly over the last thirty years. A Kyle woman's gardening experience is the exception rather than the rule: "We plant our own garden and things, and that really helps. I don't think people realize how much they can save just by having their own garden."

Many Lakotas today are well aware of their growing dependence on cash rather than land. They contrast their relationship to the land with that of previous generations. Those in their fifties and older describe their parents' or grandparents' occupation as being "self-sufficient," which meant some combination of gardening, hunting, and gathering. Many reminisce that large gardens were common when they were growing up. One Antelope woman recalls that her parents, who lived on the land of a rancher her father worked for in the late 1920s, always had a few cows and a big garden. "When I was a little girl," an elder woman from Rosebud remembers, "everybody lived on their land and with a garden. You didn't need cash then. People used to live in their log houses, which were warm. All they had to get was their gallon of kerosene. And there were hardly any heart attacks then or any stress, like thirty and forty years ago, because they'd just go to town to get their kerosene and their groceries, and they'd have their garden and some would have chickens." Despite intense poverty on the reservations during the 1920s and 1930s, contemporary people look back to those years with nostalgia. "Back in my parents' generation," a Kyle man recalls wistfully, "self-sufficiency was possible then for them, but not anymore." Indeed, in 1917, out of a population of approximately 1,500 Lakota families, 951 families owned stock as a partial means of support, 219 were using milk cows, and 750 were cultivating an average of twenty-three acres each of land for food (FARC Rosebud A-436, 8/23/17:15,29).

Boarding schools and government training programs also have promoted a cash rather than a subsistence economy on the reservations. Government boarding schools, as mentioned earlier, stressed the importance of vocational training, wage work, and other concepts related to a cash-based economy (Adams 1995:22; Child 1998:69; Ellis 1996:11; Littlefield 1993:43). Government training programs consistently encouraged Lakotas to work for wages rather than strictly for subsistence. For example, in 1933, an Indian Division of the Civilian Conservation Corp ("CCC-ID") was created under BIA supervision, extending the public works program to reservations. CCC-ID jobs in the 1930s and early 1940s became a popular labor outlet for the men of Rosebud and Pine Ridge. By 1942, some

74 percent of employable men in Rosebud had been on the payroll of the CCC-ID at one time or another (Bromert 1978:340–41, 344; Macgregor 1946:49; Szasz 1977:372; Useem, Macgregor & Useem 1943:2). The CCC-ID's regular cash income allowed a growing number of Lakota families more access to the consumer market (Mekeel 1936:10).

At the same time, because the CCC-ID projects took place away from their home communities, Lakota men were prevented from pursuing their customary short-term and seasonal subsistence activities. More families became dependent on cash income. When the CCC-ID was dismantled in 1942, the unprecedented migration of Lakota men to join the military and to work in war industry jobs in urban centers may have been a result, at least in part, of the need for more money to purchase a longer list of new consumer goods (E. Deloria 1944:94–95).

The federal Indian relocation program of the 1950s and 1960s also helped weave a cash economy into Lakotas' lives. The program encouraged natives to travel to urban centers to receive training and to work (Neils 1971:46–57). Participants in the relocation program were exposed to a more fully commodified urban existence in which money was essential to all aspects of life. Such was the experience of an Oglala woman who relocated in 1965 to California, where her husband was trained in auto bodywork: "The government helped us with housing; we got a stipend every week for groceries and clothing. Then he worked as a janitor at the naval base for four years. The government helped us for one year, and then we were on our own. He made good money, $700 every two weeks, but our apartment was $350 every two weeks. It was a hotel at the naval compound. It was cement and I hated it because we lived on the second floor and it was full of roaches. It wasn't even a good place. And it was high-priced food, everything was expensive." A woman from Kyle experienced a similar blend of bills and commodification when she and her husband were relocated to California: "The government bought us furniture and they found us a three-bedroom apartment, to help us get started. But the bills were high up there, really high. We have to pay water, garbage, parking space for your car, and a three-bedroom apartment we paid $350 a month, so most of that money we made goes on bills. Over there it was tough."

Although the amounts of money are still small by national standards, Lakota households need more and more cash to make ends meet. The reasons for their growing dependence are many and rooted in history, as we have seen. But this economic process is not relentless. Lakota values and beliefs are at work putting a brake on the engine of constantly increasing consumerism.

Avoiding Cash the Lakota Way

As we have seen, Lakotas use household, extended family, and community networks to obtain traditional items, clothing, plumbing, carpentry,
hair cutting, babysitting, car repairs, and other services, paying not in
cash but rather through some form of short- or long-term reciprocation.
Community forms of generosity such as giveaways and public meals also
work to reduce the need and opportunity for individuals to accumulate
cash savings or spend money on personal consumption.

The frequent purchase of goods through rummage sales, auctions,
and other secondhand sales also helps minimize the amount of cash
needed for household consumption. Rummage sale notices decorate the
grocery stores, churches, and electricity poles throughout the year but
most heavily in summer. The Pine Ridge radio station airs the "KILI
Swap Shop," which advertises everything from car windshields to fancy-
dance bustles, usually offered for cash or trade. Churches and community
groups hold rummage sales of items donated by off-reservation congre-
gations or nonprofit organizations to help local people find affordable
goods. Several Rosebud ladies joked to me about their recent wardrobe of
clothes from the "St. Thomas's Boutique." One elderly Rosebud woman
recited the prices of all her furniture, the bulk of which were secondhand
purchases or gifts.

Rummage sales are also held by households as a way of raising cash
for short-term needs. One St. Francis woman gives an example: "A friend
of mine is going to Disney World, and she needed to make some [store
credit] payments, so she started selling secondhand stuff." Family yard
sales are also common, and many go to them, old and young. An Antelope woman acknowledges with some amusement: "We go to yard sales
so often, when my daughter plays Barbies, they play yard sale."

Tribal natural resources also provide a hedge against cash needs. There
are still limited public use rights on tribal lands that provide low- or
no-cost hunting and gathering opportunities for subsistence. The tribe
charges well below national-market prices for hides and parts used in
craft work. Tribally managed herds of buffalo, deer, and elk supply meat,
hides, sinew, bones, hoofs, teeth, and skulls for a wide range of deco-
rative, food, and ceremonial uses. The uncle of a Porcupine man works
for the tribe to manage the elk population. "They let him go in and thin
the herd and make sure the herd is okay," the nephew reports. "I don't
know what they do with it. I suppose there is a big waiting list for getting
one of those elk, because people really use the hide and meat." Unlike
some other tribes, which emphasize wild game for tourism, Pine Ridge

views wildlife as a subsistence resource for Lakotas. Pine Ridge provides hunting permits to tribal members only, with occasional exceptions. The results of hunting, gathering, and horticulture are obtained with minimal cash and are shared freely among extended family and community members. A Kyle man who makes male headdresses called roaches illustrates this sharing: "I have a nephew who, if he hunts a porcupine, will save the hair for me, for my roaches, and this year if he catches one, he'll give the porcupine with the quills to me to prepare."

Some Lakotas attribute their low level of cash-based consumption to distinctive cultural beliefs and values that encourage a different view of materialism and consumerism from that found in the dominant society. An Antelope businesswoman makes this difference particularly clear: "I noticed when I was in Chicago, that the people there were all so into the materialism, the dress and the shopping, and I just couldn't help wondering what it all meant, what good was all that stuff if no one even looked happy or had time to enjoy life, they were working so hard to get more things. I didn't really care for it much."

There is a spiritual underpinning to the Lakotas' generosity and indifference to materialism and the accumulation of wealth. According to one Lakota spiritual leader: "Trees don't need to compete with each other or fight over who is better. It's the same with our sacred trees, which are our families. Never rise above or fall below your pipe. Ego or self-hatred makes you miss the spiritual energy that travels through all the relatives of the creator."

Accepting a lower standard of living than that of non-Indians living in border towns and urban areas is often viewed as a justified trade-off made willingly in exchange for the social and cultural freedoms of living within the reservation community. A Porcupine woman complains, however, that outsiders chiefly see the reservations as impoverished, even though many Lakotas are happier and doing better with little cash than Americans in wealthier communities.

Some Lakotas feel that their antimaterialist values are being undermined by outside forces such as churches and the federal government. "There are a lot of ways in which people have assimilated the values of the [Christian] church and the government," a Rosebud woman declares. "People who have the attitude that I'm better than you because my car is bigger and things like that; it's still possible to get trapped into that."

One indication of a growing interest in money is the lure of lotteries, bingo, and other forms of gaming. Starting with small local bingo halls with ten-dollar packets and state lottery tickets, gaming opportunities range up to the dollar slot machines and high-stakes poker tables at the

Prairie Winds and Rosebud Casinos, established on the reservation in the early 1990s, and at the larger casinos in Deadwood, Yankton, Flandreau, and Lower Brule. People who have no apparent disposable income are gaming alongside those with full-time jobs. Those with the good luck to win are announced in the paper and their experience discussed throughout the community.

Credit

Lakotas still need access to money. The imbalance between the level of cash available to Lakota households and their level of desired consumption means that, despite the antimaterialist disposition of many Lakotas, credit is a factor in their economic well-being. Lakota households have some avenues for obtaining formal credit for consumer goods. Credit for the purchase of cars is the most common form of commercial credit relations, particularly for used cars. Cars are important because there is no public transportation on either reservation and travel distances can be great. Mobile homes are another major item bought on credit. Given the lack of private investment in housing construction, mobile homes follow HUD housing in offering an attractive housing alternative. Both cars and mobile homes facilitate formal credit for Lakotas because they can serve as their own collateral; failure to make payments simply results in repossession by the lender. A common pattern among some border town used-car dealers is to sell a used car at an inflated price to a Lakota individual, refuse to make repairs for discovered defects, wait for one or more payments to be late, and then repossess the car to resell it again and again. A similar practice follows the large number of credit purchases for mobile homes — the same mobile home is hauled from one homesite to another and paid for several times over before it eventually becomes uninhabitable and unsellable.

Some local merchants permit a limited amount of goods and services to be purchased on store credit. "Because a lot of people are getting by on one monthly check basis," a Kyle businesswoman concludes, "they need a real layaway plan to get the things they and their kids need." Interestingly, those most likely to repay store credit seem to challenge stereotypical expectations. According to several small business people, Lakotas receiving public assistance were the best credit risks. "What's funny is when I give credit to those on Aid for their car repairs," a Rosebud businessman told me, "they find a way to pay me back within a month, but those with the fancy clothes and the jobs, they're the ones that will burn you, saying 'Oh, I got to go to Sioux Falls,' or 'I got this or that to pay for,' and can't make it. It was true when I worked for someone else in Mission that sold used cars. If it was folks on Aid, I wouldn't even require a down payment because they always made their payments. It was the ones with jobs that always ended up getting their cars repoed."

Other forms of consumer credit typical in non-Indian communities are difficult for reservation residents to obtain. Although many own real property, it is commonly allotted land held in trust by the federal government and therefore is unattractive to banks as security for credit. Even those families that have purchased their homes through the HUD home-ownership program do not have the access to credit that other home-owners enjoy. A Rosebud woman living in such a home explains: "Around here it's so hard to get any kind of credit unless you have collateral. So like when you buy a car, they use that for collateral. But if you need money for something else, you know it's really hard. Like my house, they don't even consider that for collateral because it's on tribal land. So it's really hard to get any kind of funding like that."

Alternative forms of lending and borrowing within the Lakota communities can at times offer a limited way of accessing some credit. This informal lending network makes credit available without subjecting the borrowers to the interest rates, mainstream conformity, and foreclosures that characterize commercial world-system bank loans. Informal lending occurs between individuals as a friend or family member asks another to "make a loan." It is a fairly common practice. As a Rosebud woman told me: "People ask to borrow. I owe a friend one hundred dollars." A Wanbli woman admits that within her community, "I would borrow and lend say five or ten dollars with people from around here, that's pretty common. Some will even lend up to four hundred dollars a month."

Informal lending is not without its problems and tensions. Lakotas are sometimes hesitant to reveal their economic status to avoid creating the impression that they have cash that others might ask to borrow. The failure to repay causes other anxieties. Relatives most frequently request loans of cash and are the most difficult to turn down because of kinship obligations. Repayment of loans from family members is uncertain and often never occurs. "When you give a relative a hundred dollars," a Manderson man told me, "you don't expect to get it back, it's a gift." Another woman complains: "I gave up giving money to relatives. I can't afford it."

Those who are in the best position to encourage payment of a personal loan are blood relatives. Families living within the *tiyóšpaye* system are ideally expected to listen to their elders. Some attribute the failure to repay loans to an erosion of the traditional values associated with the *tiyóšpaye.* The Lakota owner of a small grocery store with a large amount of bad debt from extensions of credit sees the lack of economic responsibility as lessening Lakota cultural values: "We have four thousand dollars out in credit to people who haven't paid us back. I think that mode of thinking comes from working with outsiders, like with the guys from our community, they owe me money but they don't think anything about it or what it does to our business. If we kept with the *tiyóšpaye* system, we would be able to collect a lot better. There would be an elder of each family that would see to it that the debts were paid. People wouldn't want to look bad to their elder grandma."

The force of one Lakota custom contributes to present-day credit difficulties. If people have difficulty meeting their obligations, they traditionally expect a certain amount of leniency from community members to save them from the embarrassment of admitting their shortcomings. It is therefore often more difficult for local residents to collect loan repayments from their own community members; outsiders tend to be repaid more readily to confirm that the individual was responsible for himself. Where leniency is not possible, avoidance is another method used to save face until an obligation can be met. In one instance, an Oglala community member owed money to his peer lending group. "He hides from everyone," an acquaintance confides. "He won't open his door if he is home, and if he sees anyone coming, he takes off."

Hocking personal items is another method used to meet short-term capital needs. Certain stores are known for accepting items in hock. One man sold painted earrings to get his pickup truck out of hock. Lakota individuals with cash would be approached to hold items as collateral for a small personal loan. A dozen little league baseball gloves were hocked for twenty dollars, and four Indian blankets brought fifteen dollars. The theory is that the collateral is worth so much more than the cash received that the money will surely be repaid. The reality is the personal items are rarely retrieved. As one Antelope woman noted: "I'm such a sucker. I always think they're going to come back for these things. Like twenty dollars for all these baseball gloves, I thought sure he'd have to come after them for the next game, but he never did."

Lakota small business owners and microenterprise producers commonly express the attitude that debt should be avoided. An Oglala seamstress notes: "To me, I don't believe in borrowing a large amount of money. If I'm going to have a large amount of money, I want it to be mine, but not borrowing. I really don't want to owe anybody. Like I don't want to get into a big old debt and not be able to get out of it." A Wanbli beader agrees: "I think a lot of people are afraid of the responsibility of paying back a loan."

Many of those I spoke with preferred to self-finance their enterprise, even if it extended the time it took to become operational. "I'm not the sort to ask for money," confesses a small-scale businessman from Antelope: "I'd just as soon work to save it up. Do a little job here and there, just save that money, do the next one and save, and use that money without having to take a loan. I just don't want to hear it, because I know once you're borrowing money, you've got a liability, that's all I'm thinking is you've got to pay this thing back. If you don't pay this back, things are going to happen to you, and not that you don't want to pay it back, but that's all that much more added pressure to have to stay in business." Even the larger Lakota small businesses, with gross sales in excess of $100,000 per year, shared an aversion to credit. "My advice is, don't borrow unless you absolutely have to," a jewelry storeowner from Mission explains. "I had to take out a bank loan, but only for the trailer house. I built up an inventory, started with seventy-five dollars worth of earrings, and ended up with seven thousand dollars inventory at the end of the year." Some of those involved in agriculture expressed similar concerns. "I made money in cattle because I never did owe any money on it," one Lakota rancher told me. "I didn't take any FHA or FMHA financing, so I wasn't into the loan and remortgaging rat race forever like so many of the ranchers around here. The animals we ran were all ours, and whatever we made on them went back into our pockets. Credit is what brings the business down. Five to ten years ago, they were foreclosing on everybody, but if you were debt free, you could make money in cattle."

Yet many small Lakota businesses and microenterprises need loans to compete. Most felt that more capital was required to make their enterprises successful. As one mechanic shop owner from Rosebud notes: "I need operating capital. I have no money for supplies or parts on hand, so I have to wait and order after the call to use them, and it takes a long time to get them." "I don't have the capital for the initial inventory," echoes a Lakota computer consultant. "I'd just as soon have that money for backing before I got into the bidding, so if I was awarded, I'd have the stuff on hand and could ship it immediately."

Despite their smaller size and more informal structure, Lakota microenterprises also require operating capital. Local or regional events such as powwows or Indian art shows provide potentially lucrative opportunities for sales. Aside from sales, art shows often award cash prizes for the best work in various categories of artistic or craft items, such as paintings, quilts, and beadwork. Although such periodic events attract a larger

Oglala Sioux tribal offices, headquarters for tribal self-government on the Pine Ridge Indian Reservation.

Wakpamni District Office, one of the headquarters for local government on the Pine Ridge Indian Reservation. The office was constructed during the 1960s as part of the federal government's Community Action Program.

An example of HUD cluster housing on the Pine Ridge Indian Reservation.

Traditional items, such as beadwork and dance outfits, are often made for direct family use rather than for barter or sale.

Community ceremonial honoring events often include giveaways, in which gifts are distributed to all those attending.

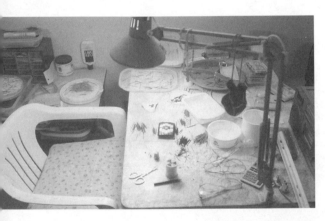

Households can engage in home-based microenterprise, such as porcupine quill work, without needing substantial equipment or cash to start.

There is a local, national, and international market for large beadwork items such as these cuffs and armbands.

Families often work together in home-based production, such as quilting.

Because they lack formal retail space, some microenterprise producers use stands at powwows and other community events as sales outlets.

Some Lakota-owned small businesses sustain the overhead of formally operating a store.

The Lakota Fund, which provides loans and technical assistance for small businesses and microenterprises on the reservation, constructed the Lakota Trade Center to provide sales space as well as meeting and training facilities to stimulate enterprise activities.

he Lakota Fund provides a sales outlet for local microenterprise producers.

The Rosebud Casino is a Rosebud tribal enterprise creating jobs and some revenue to stimulate the local economy.

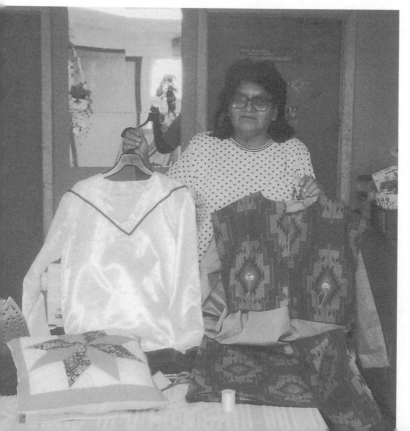

Lakota styles and pref
ences are often expres
through home-based
duction.

pool of potential buyers than is usually the case on the reservation, they can be expensive for microenterprises. In addition to transportation costs to get to an event, there is often an up-front fee of $150 to $500 for setting up a table to sell items. In order to justify the cost of participating, microenterprises need a fairly substantial inventory of completed items on hand, a requirement that in turn necessitates greater investments in materials and delaying local sales in hopes of charging potentially higher prices at the regional event.

Those Lakota business people and microenterprise producers who willingly or reluctantly accept that working capital is essential to compete are nonetheless largely shut out from commercial credit markets. Many in fact are forced to finance their ventures through personal funds or loans from relatives (Junglas & Barringer 1989:7–9). Among the owners of thirty-five small businesses interviewed for this book, 44 percent did not believe they could receive a commercial loan. If judged by the characteristics commonly used by banks, such as collateral, credit history, current work status and work history, educational background, and financial recordkeeping, many reservation small businesses and most microenterprises do not qualify for credit under a standard debt contract (Mushinski & Pickering 1996:152–56). A study of sixty-five microenterprise producers on the Rosebud Reservation shows that only seven received a bank loan and three were awarded government loans or grants (Junglas & Barringer 1989:7–9).

Collateral was often mentioned by small business people as the chief problem in the search for finance capital. As with consumer credit, the real property held by many Lakota small business owners is allotted land held in trust by the federal government and therefore unattractive to banks. Even small business owners in possession of unrestricted land within reservation borders find banks unwilling to risk pursuing foreclosure in tribal court, where jurisdiction is likely to reside. Bankers, who want to work within a system that operates under the same laws that protect their capital from other noncommodified considerations, fear that social and cultural factors outside the debt contract will influence tribal court decisions (Skari 1995:94–95).

Lakota ranchers face similar challenges when applying for credit. They need finance capital to meet the costs of land leases, machinery, livestock, and grain to make a ranching enterprise profitable. One man was running a small hog farm and needed only a small loan to buy hogs at an auction, but he confronted a hierarchy of eligibility for agricultural loan programs:

> My husband never was in any of the revolving loan funds with the Bureau. He was in Farmers Home Administration and then he graduated to Production Credit, and they're real prejudiced because there are like only three or four Indians that have graduated to that program, through the bank. You know how you graduate, like with FHA after seven years you should be self-sufficient and then they don't want to keep you anymore, they want you to move on to Production Credit in Winner, but with Production Credit it was real bad in Winner, with corruption and kickbacks, and there's hardly any Indians that made it that far. Then after you're with Production Credit so long, you have to go to the bank.

Without easy access to loans, Lakota farmers have been unable to participate in the booming technological and biotechnological innovations in agricultural inputs to which farmers in adjoining nonreservation areas have had access (Parman 1971:56).

A lack of education and training plays a role in inhibiting some Lakotas from applying for institutionalized loans. A quill worker from Potato Creek wanted to apply for a small loan, she said, "but I couldn't do it. Too much paperwork and I don't have enough education background, so they're asking me all the quills and needles and thread and whatever I need, so I started to do that and I can't get any help. So I said wait until my little girl gets education and then she can help me. But she's not interested in what I'm doing, so I just kind of lack on that." A man from Antelope just starting in small business confronts a similar problem. "There is funding out there for business," he told me: "I could go out and write up the whole business plan and apply for it, but I don't really care for forms. If you pull out some of those forms, like for a projection for two or three years, for me, I need to get some help just in doing the forms. And especially to talk to somebody with knowledge, you can talk to like at a bank here, spouting all this interest rate and this and that, it just loses me after a while."

Where commercial credit has fallen short, the federal government has attempted to step in. Several federal government credit programs were created in the late 1970s and early 1980s to supply capital to individual Indian-owned small businesses. These programs include the BIA Indian Business Development Grants and the Small Business Administration (SBA) Minority Small Business and Capital Ownership Development Contracts (Snipp and Summers 1992:173; U.S. Small Business Administration 1990:188–89, 195–96). The BIA grant, referred to as a 25/75 grant, can be used to pay up to one-quarter of new business expenses. It often takes a year or more to get a grant approved, a lag that sometimes breaks an otherwise sound deal.

In addition to gross underfunding, the major shortcoming of these federal business capital programs has been their emphasis on large loans. Because of the extensive application requirements for these programs, larger loans are justified as being more effective than smaller loans, whose dollar amount would be less than the related transaction costs.

Such large loans, however, are out of step with the predominant level of economic activity on Pine Ridge and Rosebud. For example, the SBA defines a small business in terms of millions of dollars, whereas most of the businesses in Pine Ridge and Rosebud are defined in terms of thousands of dollars or less (U.S. Small Business Administration 1990:9–10, 188–89, 196). Consequently, only a limited number of Indian-owned businesses have grown sufficiently large to manage the paperwork and service the debt load required by these programs. One Lakota businessman complains, "These programs just are not oriented to the Lakota way of thinking."

Similar criticisms have been expressed about government agricultural loan programs. Legislation and regulations for BIA agricultural loan programs have existed since the New Deal, but their limited appropriations and generally poor administration hamper their effectiveness in Rosebud and Pine Ridge. An agricultural revolving loan fund that was established during the New Deal was barely operational on Pine Ridge or Rosebud by the 1990s. Not surprisingly, Lakotas have lost confidence in federal programs of economic development, as a woman from Rosebud reflects:

> There's really no economic development program that helps around here. The BIA has loans, but they don't try to help anybody. I heard there isn't going to be any funding for the BIA agricultural loan program and that they're even going to close the program here. It's really bad. In Montana [Blackfoot Reservation], my dad had BIA loans for years, both sheep and cattle, and all my uncles, they have nice ranches, they get these loans and they have to pay them back. But here they don't keep track of the people with these loans and they don't give them to people. You have to be proven. I don't know what goes on here. In Montana they have a counselor that has a horse trailer, and you go around and count everybody's cattle and see if they have enough feed. Here there is no help or no guidance to help anybody, so everybody defaults, and there is hardly anyone who is successful.

Microenterprise lending programs have been established in Pine Ridge and Rosebud to provide alternative methods for obtaining credit. One of these is the Lakota Fund, a private nonprofit organization operating out of Kyle on the Pine Ridge Reservation whose loans support mainstream business practices and traditional arts and crafts. These programs are working to increase access to capital for smaller enterprises through peer group lending. Modeled on the Grameen Bank in Bangladesh, peer group lending makes credit available to small groups of people from the same community who lack collateral but are willing to accept liability for one another's loans. These loans range from $400 to $1,500 on a step basis, amounts appropriate for the small household incomes of Lakota microenterprise producers. Even $400 can buy raw materials and supplies in bulk, such as cloth, beads, and food ingredients, and capital goods such as sewing machines, cash registers, microwaves, and air compressors. The Lakota Fund also maintains a small business loan program for collateralized loans that banks in border towns hesitate to make.

In credit, as in other aspects of their economy, Lakota businesses, microenterprises, families, and individuals find a set of inherent contradictions. Lakota culture enforces the value that debt is to be avoided, although some internal mechanisms help alleviate the need for credit. Yet credit is often necessary if a business is to remain competitive on and off the reservation. Access to bank loans is problematic for most Lakotas, given the mainstream measures of collateral, income, and education that make an applicant creditworthy.

5

Economic Aspects of
Lakota Social Identity

The continual creation of the modern Lakota economy is inextricably
bound up with the formation of Lakota social identities. Social identities draw on forms of difference, such as gender, race, and class, which
are crucial to understanding who has access to economic resources and
opportunities and how economic returns are redistributed within and
among households and communities (H. Moore 1992:135). Social identities based on ascriptive characteristics or "naturalized" cultural conventions form the basis of power relations and institutionalized inequalities
locally, regionally, and nationally.

Within Lakota households, gender identities have economic implications in terms of negotiating strengths, expectations, and access to resources. Among households, the pseudobiological, pseudoethnic identities of full-bloods and mixed-bloods are connected to sometimes serious
conflicts over the political and economic future of the Lakotas. "Official" markers of identity, such as tribal membership, also have an impact
on economic access and opportunity. Racial identities, used by many in
South Dakota to define the relations between Indians and non-Indians,
have far-reaching economic consequences for the Lakotas. Finally, the
problem of alcoholism provides one example of how negative social identity and frustrated economic potential are intertwined within the reservation periphery of the world economy.

Gender

Viewed from the perspective of the household, women might appear to
be more prominent in Lakota society. Many Lakota households consist
only of women with children. According to the 1990 U.S. census, 33 percent of households in Pine Ridge and 35 percent in Rosebud had female
household heads with no husband. Teenage mothers, mature unmarried
mothers, divorced women, and grandmothers are all involved in the care
of young children. Because women are frequently solely responsible for

the care of children, those who also participate in wage labor contribute overall longer hours of work than Lakota men. Clusters of female cousins and sisters often support one another or form temporary households together, receiving more certain assistance from brothers and uncles than from boyfriends and husbands.

Lakota men often must choose between leaving the reservation to find wage work or being an unemployed drain on their economically precari-ous families (Albers 1982:257, 262–63; Albers 1983:188–89, 196, 198–99, 208–10; Albers 1985:122–23; Ortiz 1979:71). Some men who make little or no economic contribution to the family's welfare have been pressured by relatives to leave (Albers 1985:122–23). Adding to the instability and lack of connection between Lakota men and their households is the fact that many men have two families—one set of children from a relationship they had in their twenties and another from their thirties or forties. Other men have a string of children from different shorter-term relationships.

Despite their economic importance and crucial familial roles, the over-all social status of Lakota women is generally considered subordinate to that of men. Their subordinate position is tenuous, however, requir-ing constant confirmation by Lakota men. Humor is the most prevalent method by which women are reminded of their proper place as wives, not leaders. Domestic violence is another, unfortunate method for main-taining inequality between men and women.

Male domination through physical abuse is prevalent and is of great concern to reservation women. Work environments for women can be poisoned by the excessive jealousy of some men. Violence by fathers against daughters often works to keep young women from looking for employment outside the home. Young Lakota women living on the reser-vation for the first time, who were born while their parents or grand-parents were living in urban areas, are more willing to question gender relations and are more aware of alternatives to physical abuse in relation-ships. Sometimes, though, even these women end up in abusive relation-ships.

Attempts by Lakota women to improve their economic options by seeking higher education sometimes provoke violent encounters with their male partners. One woman who worked with male batterers ob-serves: "Many times men are insecure and put up obstacles to women working or getting training because they're afraid that either she'll wake up and leave him, or find somebody better at the college, so her efforts to improve herself often lead to escalations of violence. A big portion of women who start at the college end up divorced or single again if they stick to their plans and graduate." Separation from a negative relationship can, however, create an opportunity for women to return to higher education. "I was in a battering relationship," a woman from Porcupine told me, "and when I got out of that, I went back to college."

Given the unrelenting economic and social pressures on Lakotas, love relationships and the solidarity of households can be extremely vulnerable. Many women recounted stories to me of being left by an ex-spouse for a new relationship. Feelings of bitterness, betrayal, and mistrust between and among men and women are quite common. According to a woman from Antelope, the fragility of love relationships fosters distrust even among women: "We have a women's group, and that's the main thing we've had to work on is learning to trust each other, being able to say what's bothering us and why. It's because of what goes on around here. People really get bent out of shape because there are women who will go after other women's husbands. So it takes a lot of work."

Some Lakota women feel that the current gender inequality on the reservation is a product of Euro-American influences. Returning to Lakota cultural traditions, they argue, would improve the conditions of reservation women.

There are noticeable gender dimensions to wage work on the reservations. Many Lakota women feel that they confront a glass ceiling in the workplace. Men nominally head several institutions on the reservations, but women with less prestigious titles and lower pay do most of the work. For example, men occupy prominent positions in Lakota tribal governments, but the follow-through work is being carried out by women in assistant, administrative, and secretarial positions. Tribal chairmen, councilmen, college presidents, board chairmen, and chief judges are overwhelmingly male. Given the predominance and prestige of tribal government jobs, this gender discrepancy threatens to severely curtail women's access to productive resources on the reservations. Although women are able to get jobs for themselves, they are less able than men to direct who will be given other positions. Consequently, Lakota women may have more knowledge than men of the real workings of tribal government, but they have less political and economic power.

Other employment is also shaped by gender. Most temporary and seasonal positions, comprising more than half the wage work available on both reservations, are weighted toward men. Men dominate construction work, agricultural labor, carpentry, and plumbing. In local economies with a strong service sector, as in the border towns with extensive tourism, there tend to be more jobs for women, such as temporary seasonal work as maids in motels during the tourist season. Within reservation boundaries, tourism is much less important, so many Lakota women work as part-time cooks for the school year or temporary cooks for summer programs.

Several women also pointed out that the structure of Lakota organizations is affected by gender. "There is still a problem with sexism within the communities," a woman from Rosebud acknowledges, "especially those that are called more traditional. There is an attitude that you need a man to be on the board or to do the job, and like other forms of internalized oppression, even the women start to think that way." Lakota non-governmental organizations accommodate some leadership roles for women, such as executive director or member of a board of directors. For example, the White Buffalo Calf Women's Society explicitly includes women on its board of directors.

A gender-based division of wage labor positions began early during the emergence of reservation life. Lakota women were expected to follow the model of mainstream white society and clean, cook, or sew. At the boarding schools, Lakota women were employed to sew the garments for children to wear, work in the kitchens, and do laundry (FARC Rosebud A-436, 8/23/17:24). An elderly Antelope woman was an aide at a BIA dorm for twenty-eight years, taking care of girls at the boarding school. "I started sewing when I first went to work at the boarding school," she remembers. "We made clothes for the students, shirts, dresses, and nightgowns and like that, and in the summertime when there were no students, that was our job."

In the early decades of the twentieth century, many Lakota men worked for non-Indian ranchers while Lakota women cooked for the hired men. A woman from St. Francis recalls her childhood in the 1940s when her father worked as a ranch hand and her mother cooked for forty-odd temporary hands who hayed the fields: "They had this trailer house, it was really just like a house only it was high up on wheels, and it was as wide as the living room, and in one corner we used to cook, and the rest was tables, and the men would sit on benches. They dragged that to different places where the men had to work. That was a lot of cooking, so you better be a good cook." At that time, when a Lakota couple worked for the same agricultural employer, non-Indians assumed that Lakota men controlled the finances of the household. By the same token, women were expected to need less pay and less cash because they were supposedly relying on a man for the bulk of their support.

Federal government programs for the reservations often help institutionalize gender bias. Early in the reservation period, such programs promoted the dependence of Lakota women on men as the Lakota economy became incorporated into the U.S. market system. Western European ideas of property rights challenged Lakota beliefs that the direct producer is the owner of his or her products (Albers 1983:182–84, 187, 190, 194; Hurt 1987:144). Women were generally excluded from federal training programs for Lakota ranchers. Women were also treated differently when tribal lands were allotted to individuals. Allotments were made to all reservation members, but the size varied according to age, gender, and marital status. Lands were distributed to the heads of nuclear family households, presumed to be male by the federal government at that time. Male household heads received larger allotments and were often given the prerogative to decide where the land holdings of other family members would be located (Albers 1985:118–19).

Nevertheless, more and more Lakota women are entering a traditional bastion of male dominance: the military. Lakota women enlisted in the service during World War II, Korea, and Vietnam, and young women continue to enlist to gain training and a sense of independence. As one woman from Wanbli recalls: "I was in the service from 1978 to 1981, before I got married. I was in the service in California, South Carolina, and Arizona. I was trained as a field radio operator. I was about the only female in that unit. We were doing desert training; it was pretty rough to make it through, but I held my own."

As in other peripheral areas of the global economy, Lakota women play a larger part in the informal economy of the reservations than men (Browne 1997; Tice 1995; Ward 1985). Women tend to have more skills and opportunities for microenterprise and household production, moving fairly easily between the formal and informal sectors of production. Both men and women are involved in beading and quilling, but quilting and sewing is predominantly a female activity. Eighty percent of the beaders I spoke with were women. Women make clothing for family members and sew to make extra money. As the primary caretakers of children, Lakota women are able to combine babysitting with some form of microenterprise, such as beading, quilting, food catering, hair styling, or sewing. Women also predominate in gardening, canning, and housework, as in previous generations. "My mom did a lot of work at home, sewing and cooking," a woman from Porcupine remembers about the 1930s, "and at the time I was growing up we had to have our own garden, our own vegetables that she canned and stored them in the cellar, and that was her food for the winter. That's the way it was then." Another Porcupine woman recalls similar women's activities in the early 1950s: "In those days, my mom and aunts all taught me how to do things with my hands, and I had to help with gardening and canning and keeping the household. There wasn't any time to sit around."

In an environment where jobs are limited for Lakota women, these types of informal economic activities provide needed financial support for them and their families. Because of their skills, primary responsibility within households, and experience performing many types of work, women are more easily able than men to move fluidly back and forth from wage work to household production (Boris and Prugl 1996: 11; Ward 1993:54, 59).

Among Households: Blood, Class, and Membership

Lakota households also serve as the fulcrums for social tensions within the community, tensions that both are informed by and spill over into the economic realm. Some of these tensions can be traced to differences in the degree to which households are incorporated into the world economy.

Mixed-Bloods and Full-Bloods

Some households in indigenous communities readily embrace the social relations and material culture that accompany prolonged interaction with the world economy. Sometimes that embrace is rejected. Others might be more inclined to stay the course, keeping the visual and social intrusions of the world system to a minimum as much as possible. Sometimes those intrusions cannot be avoided. There is great variability; some households are able to control the extent of their incorporation, while others are not.

As in many American Indian communities, such a spectrum of incorporation has been mischaracterized within Pine Ridge and Rosebud as constituting two opposing groups — mixed-bloods and full-bloods. Two factors play a role in the construction of these ethnic social identities. Given the association with blood, biology is the more prominent and seemingly natural component. However, it is the second factor, a person's cultural behavior (economic, social, political, and religious), that is often more determinative of which ethnic identity Lakotas ascribe to a particular individual (Wax, Wax and Dumont 1964:29–30). Academics have characterized full-bloods as economically "isolated" impediments to economic development but as culturally "authentic" (Macgregor 1946; Roberts 1943; Useem, Macgregor & Useem 1943) and, by contrast, mixed-bloods as economically "modern" but as culturally diminished or compromised (Meyer 1990:332).

In reality, the distinction is not a simple dichotomy based on blood but rather involves a complex spectrum of individual experiences and household choices centering on the opportunities for and receptivity to the system and culture of the world economy. Naturalizing the differences between full-bloods and mixed-bloods as genetic helps impel and articulate the internal economic, social, and political discourse on difficult reservation issues. Points of view on how to mediate the pressures of the world economy to preserve and advance Lakota culture while improving local living conditions are often valued or discounted based on the heritage of individuals rather than the validity of their arguments. The appropriation of the mixed-blood/full-blood classification scheme masks the role that outside economic and political interests have played in its establishment (Wax, Wax and Dumont 1964:30–36; see Meyer 1990: 332). The complex tensions between culture and the world economy become reduced to a simple issue of blood quantum.

In general, the factionalism embodied in the full-blood and mixed-blood categories represents conflicting views about the efforts needed to assert control over the economic, political, and cultural trajectories of the reservations. Lakota history is replete with dichotomous parties — full-bloods and mixed-bloods, traditionals and progressives, renegades and treaty chiefs — struggling for generations to determine the proper balance between cultural tradition and participation in the world economy. Both sides are Lakota, operating on the basis of contemporary Lakota culture and values. According to many full-bloods, greater diligence is required to preserve Lakota culture. Many mixed-bloods accept, in varying degrees, outside economic incorporation and cultural influence and focus instead on seeking ways to increase the economic, political, and social benefits resulting from that incorporation and influence. The conflicts between these perspectives turn on the methods for accomplishing their priorities and the strategies for responding to outside forces. In general, those Lakotas considered full-bloods resist world-system involvement to the greatest degree possible in order to limit its inevitable exploitation of Lakota people and culture. Mixed-bloods tend to embrace world-system involvement in order to increase the extent it can help Lakota people and culture.

BIOLOGY OR BEHAVIOR

The Lakotas' continuing attention to the quantity of an individual's Indian blood as a basis for ascribing social identities is rooted in their reservation history. Under pressure from the United States government, tribal governments needed to define their members in an acceptable way. As part of establishing tribal governments under the Indian Reorganization Act in the 1930s, each Lakota "tribe" was required to create a roster of members as of a particular date and to define the qualifications for membership for subsequent generations in terms of percentage of tribal blood quantum. For example, in Rosebud, a census roll was made in 1935. To be enrolled, a person must be listed on the 1935 census roll or be a descendant of an original member and must have at least one-fourth or more of Rosebud Sioux Indian blood (Grobsmith 1981:28; Nagel 1996:22, 90–91). An elder man from Kyle explains the impact of the government's role in using race for enrollment: "People will look at the *iyéska* [mixed-blood] and blame their white part for what goes wrong, like on the board or on the tribal council, but it's the government that made things work out that way, not because you're white or Indian."

Traditionally, Lakota identity turned more on appropriate behavior and family membership than on biological ancestry. Individuals from other tribes or non-Indians were adopted into Lakota families as a result of warfare, capture, and other circumstances (Hassrick 1964:110–12; Walker 1982:32, 42, 63). Many Lakotas today continue to express the sentiment that it should not matter whether a person has white ancestors or not as long as he or she behaves like a good Lakota person. When issues of economic and political power intensify among Lakotas, however, race is thrown into relief. A man with a white father and a Lakota mother admits, "When I'm in the white world, all they see is an Indian. And yet when I'm here, people tell me I belong in the white world. So there's no right place for me."

It is crucial to realize, however, that the reasons given by Lakotas for calling a person mixed-blood or full-blood are usually not to explain ancestry but to explain how they behave. Although the biology and assumed stereotyped behavior of an individual coincide in some situations, there are myriad other situations in which they do not. For example, large families are often automatically identified as mixed-bloods. Before the reservations were established, Lakota cultural norms worked to limit the number of children a couple would have. Parents were expected to abstain from sex until children were weaned at age three or four (Hassrick 1964: 314). During the early reservation period, some families maintained these practices, but others began having larger numbers of children. BIA household censuses from the 1910s, 1920s, and 1930s indicate that there were both full-blood and mixed-blood couples with more than two children (FARC Pine Ridge 32–2, 1904–1914; FARC Rosebud A-319). The increase in the number of children was related to pressures from a number of media of incorporation, such as membership in the Catholic church, marriage to non-Indians, and the labor demands of farming and ranching. These pressures applied regardless of biological background and were related

more to the increasing engagement of Lakota society with the world system and the varying responses of Lakota families to that experience.

ETHNICITY AND CLASS

In one sense, the ethnic identities associated with varying quantities of
Indian blood are used to stand for those who have and those who have
not. Mixed-blood and full-blood issues almost invariably turn on economic distinctions. Although Lakota values encourage generosity and
mutual support, in a context of limited goods distrust is created if one
segment of the community somehow shirks its duty of reciprocity in
favor of personal enrichment. "It's rough around here," a woman from
Manderson confides. "People in this community get stuff and they don't
share. But here they get the police involved if I get stuff, so they know it
was donated to me and not to the district." Being mixed-blood symbol-
izes both greater involvement in the outside economy and a less certain
commitment to Lakota social relations based on generosity and sacrifice for relatives. The truth of various assertions about and characteriza-
tions of mixed-blood behavior is not as important as the persistence and
vitality of the belief that such behavior exists and is associated with ethnicity.

No one on Pine Ridge and Rosebud has the financial resources to be
considered elite by national standards. A handful of Lakotas are well-
off enough to be considered wealthy by reservation standards. Although
there are a wide variety of jobs and employers, relatively few positions
offer the opportunity for promotion and salary increases beyond a fairly
limited range. Good-paying jobs start at around $20,000 a year. More
than half the wage labor positions are part-time, seasonal, or temporary.
A full 27 percent of households have no wage workers at all. Therefore,
if a Lakota is employed, especially in a full-time, year-round job, others
could be provoked into considering that person wealthy.

Lakotas do not agree about what actually constitutes the wealthy class.
Those with wage work see the small business people as wealthy; the small
business people in turn consider the government workers to be better off,
with better pay and more security for less work. Those with money tend
to be those working at government jobs, in small businesses or ranching,
or sometimes in tribal politics. It is these very activities that are stereo-
typically identified as mixed-blood occupations. People biologically of
full-blood descent, however, have been involved in ranching and tribal
government for some time. For example, in 1917, four of the five largest
acreages farmed by individual Indians were farmed by "full bloods" be-

tween thirty-eight and forty-five years of age, which meant they were all born before the formation of the reservations (FARC Rosebud A-436, 8/23/17:26).

A popular view within the reservation communities is that mixed-bloods get all the wage jobs and full-bloods have fewer opportunities. This internal sense of ethnic discrimination fosters social tensions over the survival of oneself, one's immediate family, and one's broader community. Some Lakotas attribute the presumed greater access of mixed-bloods to wage work to more acculturated behavior and experience. A Rosebud woman identifying herself as full-blood asserts: "See, with the full-bloods, when you apply for a job they tell you that you don't have the right kind of training and you don't have enough schooling, so the half-breeds come in and get all those jobs. That really happens."

Another popular Lakota explanation for mixed-blood wealth focuses on social relationships that enable economic opportunities. As mentioned earlier, Lakotas in wage positions tend to help other family members get jobs as they become available. The supposed ubiquity of this practice among mixed-bloods leads a Rosebud man to comment: "Here it's all racism and families, so for me it's easier to get jobs in the city." "Because I don't come from one of the well-known families, I don't have the same chance," complains an extremely poor young woman from Pine Ridge. Among competing small businesses, there is a common view that the business people who are least Indian have the best economic opportunities. "Indian preference is a joke," argues a Rosebud businessman. "They don't even apply it. Some may be Indian that get the BIA and tribal contracts, but just enough Indian that if they cut themselves, they'd lose all their Indian blood."

Another characteristic some Lakotas associate with mixed-blood behavior is a willing complicity in the efforts of outside interests to control the economic and political agenda of the reservation. Some have asserted that for Indian tribes in general, a class of comprador Indian elites has been formed and used by the U.S. government to authorize government and private programs that are detrimental to the real interests of the tribe. According to some Lakotas, this purported powerful class of "white Indians" uses the tribe's resources to promote the interests of the dominant white economy at the expense of the tribe, and uses Indian poverty as a means of securing government grants that wind up in the hands of local white contractors, merchants, and businessmen (Anders 1980:693–94). In ranching, the behavior that is condemned and linked to mixed-bloods is taking money from non-Indian ranchers in exchange for granting them access to leased tribal lands, after which the outsiders abuse tribal resources. There is a general perception that certain Lakotas, invariably labeled mixed-bloods, serve as fronts for non-Indian ranchers to get agricultural leases under the Indian preference program and then let beneficial interest in those lands run to non-Indians.

Profit-driven is another widespread characterization of wealthy mixed-blood behavior. Mixed-blood store owners were often described to me as the worst exploiters of Lakota microenterprises: "That mixed-blood woman with the store here, she's only paying ten dollars for baby moccasins, so she's really making out. She sells them for a whole lot more in Europe. But if people need money, they'll sell their things cheap."

The inherent economic dimension of this ethnic classification scheme has been present from the early reservation years. Associations linking ethnicity, opportunity, and economic well-being were not the sole creation of reservation residents. BIA agents kept records based on mixed-blood and full-blood distinctions (FARC Pine Ridge 32–2, 1904–1914; FARC Rosebud A-436, 8/23/17; Marquette University Library Archives 1914) and viewed mixed-bloods as more suited to participate in government economic programs. Preferences and favoritism shown to mixed-bloods by BIA employees created an atmosphere of conflict and distrust on the part of full-bloods who were excluded simply because of their heritage.

POLITICAL BEHAVIOR

Lakotas also employ ethnicity to denote who is politically conservative or liberal, as defined entirely within a reservation context. Political behavior has long played a role in the construction of mixed-blood and full-blood identities, frequently increasing the pain and paralysis of tribal politics and internal political debates. If nonracial terms were used for these opposing perspectives, the two camps would easily be interpreted as political parties, one side favoring culturally conservative approaches, the other embracing greater social change. Lakotas associated with both sides compete and are elected to tribal government. Because of the racializing of political rhetoric, some views are overwhelmed by questions about the person's ethnicity and corresponding right to an opinion on an issue. In the contemporary political context, mixed-bloods may feel discriminated against by full-bloods, particularly when it comes to voicing their views on the future of social, economic, and political conditions on the reservations. Full-bloods may cast themselves as the only "real" Lakotas entitled to participate in the discourse about maintaining appropriate Lakota behavior and tradition. The relatively recent history of the federal government's injustices against Lakotas also elevates the political rhetoric to more than just competing concepts of governance. There are critical concerns over how to respect the sacrifices of prior generations of Lakota leaders who struggled to maintain Lakota independence and sovereignty, sacrifices that Lakotas feel should not be discarded lightly.

When tribal officials are characterized as mixed-blood, they are perceived as willing to let outside interests dominate or sway their decisions. There is concern that tribal officials are susceptible to financial payoffs from outsiders eager to take advantage of tribal resources. This concern derives from a general healthy suspicion of community members who get too close to outside interests trying to bring projects to the reservation. Such inherent wariness can make some constituents quite hostile to those elected to tribal office. A disgruntled man from Pine Ridge recalls: "When I was district president, I wanted to do a buffalo commons idea, but the council was controlled by ranchers and those with an interest in the land. And the BIA and the tribe are hand-in-hand with them; it's total cronyism. That's never changed either. We tried in 1973 to get the government to change for the people, but it never has." Unfortunately, there are sufficient examples of tribal officials who use their office for personal enrichment to reinforce these suspicions. For example, after a serious car accident when patients needed to be air-lifted to Sioux Falls, the story circulated that a tribal official was given a government check to buy airstrip lights but they were never paid for and the money was never recovered. Such stories of corruption and mismanagement create lingering suspicion about the political and economic effectiveness of the tribal government and the sincerity of the individuals holding office in that government.

THE SECOND WOUNDED KNEE

The social construction of ethnic identities out of economic and political perspectives has had profound effects for Lakotas in recent decades. In the 1970s, longstanding political and economic tensions exploded at the standoff at Wounded Knee in 1973 and the incident at Oglala in 1975. At the height of the internal struggles between the American Indian Movement (AIM) and tribal government supporters, labeled "goons" by their opponents, Lakota political leaders came to recognize that both sides of the struggle contained genetic full-bloods and mixed-bloods.

The 1970s witnessed a revival and growth of Lakota tribal nationalism. Long-term tensions between the "progressive" supporters of the tribal government structures of the Indian Reorganization Act (IRA) and the "traditional" components of the Pine Ridge and Rosebud reservation communities reached a crisis in 1973–75 with the arrival of the American Indian Movement and the occupation of Wounded Knee. The American Indian Movement, although controversial, attracted outside attention to the dismal conditions of Lakotas and other Native Americans and helped revive interest and pride in tribal traditional beliefs and practices. Pine Ridge was torn between two camps. The formal tribal chairman, Dick Wilson, and his so-called goon supporters favored "economic progress through cooperation with the government," structured through the Indian Reorganization Act with BIA oversight (Dewing 1985:70–71). AIM, with its supporters from various sectors of the tribe, proclaimed itself to be more "traditional," calling attention to the tribe's violated treaty rights and warning against federal involvement in tribal affairs. Although there were racial full-bloods on both sides of this dispute, it came to be characterized by Lakotas and others as a confrontation between "mixed-blood" supporters of the federal government and "full-blood" supporters of the traditional interests of the tribe (V. Deloria & Lytle 1984:239–40; Matthiessen 1980:60–74, 129–32; M. Powers 1986:144, 150–52). The escalation of the conflict between these groups was due in large part to external enforcement by federal officials and agencies.

There were many short-term consequences to the standoff at Wounded Knee. The composition of the tribal councils began to change as the American Indian Movement and civil rights concerns became increasingly influential on Pine Ridge and Rosebud. Elders became more active in the political discourse and in tribal politics. Yet, although the physical violence of the second Wounded Knee period has largely dissipated, the divisions linger. Many Lakotas still identify others by which side they were on during that watershed crisis. Several people mentioned to me their concern over the local filming of the movie *Thunderheart* because of its potential to dredge up bad feelings that had started to settle down and be forgotten. The scars of this division continually resurfaced in the workings of the tribal government in the last years of the twentieth century. For example, the tribal council elected in Pine Ridge in April 1988 was paralyzed for months during a dispute between the council and the tribal treasurer, a conflict that was alternately characterized as an issue of the treasurer's incompetence or as a case of political retaliation against the treasurer because of her AIM affiliation (*Lakota Times,* 7/88).

The social identity of ethnicity, naturalized by the biological association of the terms *full-blood* and *mixed-blood,* continues to play a significant role in determining the perceived and actual economic and political opportunities available to Lakotas.

Tribal Identity

One of the key functions of a reservation tribal government is to determine who is eligible for enrollment as a member of the tribe. When seven independent reservations were formed from the Great Sioux Nation, this power to create citizenship and construct racial and geographical barriers around it artificially limited the ability of Lakotas to gain access to jobs and services even on the Lakota reservations. Superimposed on the historically fluid character of Lakota residence, participation, and kinship was a rigid and static system of enrollment that exists to this day. One elderly man from St. Francis recalls the effects of the reservation system on his family history: "I have land on both Pine Ridge and Rosebud because when my parents were first married, they lived in Oglala but you had to get a pass from the superintendent in order to leave the reservation boundaries. They got a pass to come over to Rosebud to visit my mom's sister, but they stayed too long and the pass expired so they just stayed. If you left the reservation and you didn't have a pass, you could get shot. So then when that allotment came in, my dad got land over in Pine Ridge and my mom got land through her sister over here."

In an effort to conserve the benefits of a tribal economy for members of the tribe, Lakotas have followed other native communities in limiting enrollment, mainly by keeping the blood-quantum requirement as high as possible. When tribes confront the possibility of reducing blood-quantum amounts from one-quarter to one-sixteenth, it is feared that people with no real association with either Lakota culture or political sovereignty could be in a position to take over and skew the tribal government away from the interests of "real" Lakota people. But because the reservations are arbitrary divisions among culturally, economically, and historically interacting members of the larger Lakota cultural unit, higher reservation blood-quantum requirements can lead to the exclusion of individuals who, from the perspective of both Lakotas and non-Indians, are legitimate tribal members.

The rules of tribal membership are determined by each tribe. In 1992 a resolution to lower the blood quantum required for Rosebud Sioux tribal membership from one-quarter to one-sixteenth Sicangu Lakota was considered but ultimately rejected. Although such a policy of allowing only "real" Sicangu to be members appears straightforward, it is in fact tremendously complex. People with only Lakota ancestors but who came from reservations other than Rosebud would not be considered full-bloods. If enough of their ancestors were from other reservations, they may not be eligible for enrollment in Rosebud. Children may be ineligible for enrollment on the basis of blood quantum, even though their families have lived for more than four generations on the same reservation and culturally have only Lakota ancestors. Given the tremendous amount of social, economic, and political interchange among the various Lakota reservations, there are real, negative consequences to enforcing these policies.

Enrollment has further implications and complications for the concept of individual identification in relation to tribal nationalism. The reservation of enrollment, of childhood, and of adult residence could be three different places or all the same place. The pressures of unemployment and welfare assistance and an attitude of flexibility in relation to divorce often lead children to live with one parent on one reservation while being enrolled with the other parent's tribe. Job preferences and family support available to one spouse might also cause children to grow up where they were not enrolled. Even though no political rights were attached to that reservation, the child would be likely to consider it "her rez" on the basis of social and emotional ties. Similar pressures of job opportunity and marriage might lead that child herself to move to another reservation as an adult (Albers 1982:255; M. Powers 1986:88–89; Walker 1982:41–44). In general, Lakotas who are born, enrolled, and live in one reservation community their entire lives tend to identify more strongly with their reservation than Lakotas who are associated with three different reservations and feel a stronger "pan-Lakota" identification (see Nagel 1996:240–43).

The issue of who is a tribal member and where has a tremendous economic effect on individuals, households, and families. One set of tensions surrounds the fact that enrolled members have an advantage when applying for tribal jobs. The greatest competition for such positions is for full-time protected jobs, and enrolled tribal members who qualify for these jobs receive preference over other Lakota applicants who are enrolled members of other tribes. Less attractive temporary and seasonal jobs, such as construction and manual labor, provide the bulk of opportunities for Lakota workers who are not enrolled tribal members. As a Rosebud woman explains: "It's hard when you're from a different tribe, because if you're from a different tribe and you live in a different place, you have a hard time finding work. My dad was from Pine Ridge and we lived in Rosebud where my mom was from, so that was his problem. I really don't think that's fair." Whereas tribal members are ensured some limited access to tribal positions, non-member Indians, even those who are lifetime residents of the reservation but are enrolled with other Lakota tribes, are ineligible for such jobs unless no local tribal member applies. One man living in Pine Ridge complained to me: "I'm enrolled in Crow Creek, so I can't get a job down here. By the time all the enrolled members sign up, the job is over." Another man was enrolled in Fort Yates but was married to a Rosebud woman and lived there with her family for more than twenty years. He was able to get only temporary positions with tribal agencies. He felt his nonmember status gave his supervisor the chance to exploit him, take credit for his work, and deprive him of benefits. Whenever a permanent position opened up, he was always passed over in favor of a tribal member.

Community tensions also surface when nonmembers are fortunate enough to receive one of the limited positions on the reservation. A Lakota woman describes such a problem in her community: "They were just trying to get rid of a nonmember ambulance driver, and yet no members ever applied for the job. When these jobs come open, there's only one or two that even apply, so I want to know where they are then. Why don't they come in then and fill out an application, rather than waiting to jump down on the nonmembers that take the initiative. It's always the hollering ones that don't apply for the positions that are posted."

One economic consequence of the Indian Self-Determination and Education Act of 1975 was the legislative enactment of Indian hiring preferences for Indian agency positions (Stubben 1994:111). The federal policy of Indian preference in employment has several angles, however. All the BIA requires at a Lakota reservation is that an employee be Indian, not necessarily Lakota. Indian people working for the BIA are part of the federal civil service system and are often confronted with the choice of working on different reservations to maintain their career paths or giving up their civil service job security in order to remain on their home reservations. One's work identity as a federal employee takes precedence over tribal identity and any desire to serve the people of one's tribe.

This issue was highlighted when the Rosebud Sioux Tribe voted in 1991 to contract with the BIA to manage its own police force. Previously, all the reservation police positions were BIA civil service positions. The chief of police was an enrolled member of the tribe and considered an outstanding officer. But keeping his job of police chief on the newly contracted tribal police force required him to give up his eighteen years of service with the federal government and lose his civil service pension. The alternative, remaining a BIA employee, meant that he would be reassigned to another reservation that had not contracted to manage its own police force.

Social Identity of Race: Indians and Non-Indians

The social identity of race can exclude certain groups from the benefits of the market economy. In Pine Ridge and Rosebud, the conflicted
social relations between Indians and non-Indians illustrate how identity,
race, and class work at the local level to perpetuate inequality. Through
individual transactions, such local social relations play out the tensions,
conflicts, and power differentials between Lakota culture and the world
economy. Being Indian or non-Indian has a profound impact on the way
the market defines the returns available from production and exchange.

Commodity Agriculture

One of the premises underlying the invasion and settling of the Dakotas
by non-Indians was that Lakotas were primitive nomads who were not
productively using the land and who needed to be forced into a sedentary
agricultural lifestyle to become civilized (Carlson 1981:8–9, 66; Hurt 1987:
152; Poole 1988:38–39, 43–44). The social identity of Indians as inferior
continues to serve, sometimes implicitly, as the basis for class formation
in South Dakota, an attitude and practice reproduced in new ways by the
non-Indian communities surrounding the reservations.

Opening the Rosebud Reservation to white settlement of "surplus"
lands in 1904 — a consequence of the Dawes Allotment Act — meant that
non-Indian ranchers and farmers became neighbors to the Lakota community (Iverson 1994:40). Interactions between Lakotas and their new
white neighbors soon erupted as economic disputes, as evinced by the
recollection of an elderly Rosebud man:

> Our grandfathers were hunters, they followed the buffalo around, but the
> government came in and wanted them to be farmers or something. So they
> divided up the land and gave 160 acres and a cow and a horse or some-
> thing. But they weren't trained to be farmers. And the white ranchers in
> the area would make up bills of sale and take the Indians' cattle, since all
> the cattle had the same BIA brand on them. But when an Indian took some
> white guy's cattle, he was hung. That went on in the '30s and '40s too, that
> wasn't just in the olden times. When I was about five years old, my uncle
> left for the white ranchers that lived next door, and he took his gun with
> him, and my aunt was crying and I asked her where he was going. He was
> going over to get his cattle back from the white guy. We had about twenty
> head in those days. I asked my aunt if they were going to shoot each other,
> and she said they might. But he came back later that night and he had his
> cows with him.

An incipient class system emerged in which Lakotas, as they became increasingly alienated from landholding, provided inexpensive labor for

non-Indians. The gradual transfer by the BIA of real and effective title to tribal lands into the hands of large-scale, non-Indian agricultural interests created a corps of Lakota agricultural workers available at low wages (Burgess 1991). Lakotas over time became the primary subsidizers of mainstream agriculture in the region.

Without easy access to capital, Lakota families frequently were forced to enter into agricultural wage work. Fifteen percent of the Lakotas I formally interviewed described their fathers' occupation as ranch hand, farmhand, or vegetable picker. A woman from Manderson, for example, remembers her agricultural life in the 1960s: "My dad worked in Wanbli and then in Scottsbluff for a farmer. We picked potatoes, and I continued on after I married picking potatoes." In some communities, more than half the Lakota families left home together to harvest potatoes in Nebraska each September (Useem, Macgregor & Useem 1943:3).

Non-Indians struggled to make a profit on agricultural commodities in the early 1900s. Inexpensive, reliable Lakota labor made local white operations profitable in ways not possible if they had had to employ full-time workers or white workers. Lakotas working as seasonal farmhands and harvesters at piece rates for non-Indian wheat, corn, and potato farmers and cattle ranchers minimized labor costs for their non-Indian agricultural employers. Non-Indian farmers and ranchers provided maintenance for Lakota workers only while they worked seasonally, leaving the Lakota community to help the laborers during the winter months. By encouraging Indians to lease their tiny parcels of land through the BIA, non-Indian operations became even more profitable as Indian lands became available for lease at below-market rates. In a few instances, Lakota men actually worked as day laborers on their own allotment parcels for white ranchers to whom the land was leased by the BIA (Carlson 1981:156–57). Yet, despite the support of banks, USDA Extension services, and state university research experiment stations, non-Indian agricultural employers were able to produce only marginal incomes with regular loss years because of bad weather conditions, crop sensitivity to local pests, and irregular growing seasons (Johnston 1948:119–22). Given these tight economic boundaries, access to flexible, low-cost labor made a crucial difference to survival and success.

Some Lakota families developed long-term relationships with white agricultural families, working to harvest their produce each year on a per row or per bushel piece rate (Useem, Macgregor & Useem 1943:3). A woman from Antelope describes such an experience in the 1930s:

> The same rancher that had this ranch at St. Francis used to have a ranch
> south of Meriman, Nebraska, and that's where my dad started working for

him, and then when they moved over here, they moved Dad over here with
them at St. Francis, so Dad worked for him most of his life. We knew that
rancher real well. In the summertime, in haying season, they had a lot of
men working for them, forty men in the summer, since they had all the
horse-drawn equipment, hayers and all, that needed men to operate them.
It was an all summer's job. It started right after the 4th of July and ended
in August. But my dad would work for him over the winter months too.
Our home was on this guy's land, about five miles from their big ranch.
When they would finish up their summer haying, the rest would go back
to their homes, and we'd go back to our home.

Many Lakotas who had committed long years to agricultural wage
work were left with no financial support in their later years. Because many
of the available farm labor activities were seasonal, part-time, or temporary, benefits for disability, retirement, unemployment, or survivors
of workers were seldom enjoyed by Lakota agricultural wage workers.
Several Lakotas described unscrupulous employers who did not record
their workers or pay their employment taxes, so their workers had no
work record even though they should have been entitled to benefits. A
man from Kyle worked as a farmhand for the same non-Indian farmer
for twenty years until he literally broke his back, "so he couldn't do
any more heavy work," his wife reports. Because the farmer never paid
into Social Security for him, he was disabled but ineligible for any work-
related Social Security benefits. Another man from Kyle was turning
sixty-five years old and had worked for one rancher for twenty-five years
and another rancher for twenty years. "I have just one more year until
I can retire and get Social Security," he told me. "One of the ranchers I
worked for wasn't paying it in, so I lost some quarters that way." Injuries
and health problems were common. A woman from Potato Creek is con-
vinced that her dad developed arthritis from all his years doing irrigation
work for a non-Indian farmer; ultimately, he died from it.

Federal government policy and practice effectively kept Lakota people
from being competitive with non-Indian agricultural interests. Early reservation agents controlled agricultural access to markets for those Lakota
families that had not left reservations for independent homesteading.
The BIA was "the most complete colonial system in the world" (Thomas
1967:70), dominating the economic as well as the political and social lives
of Lakota reservation residents (Cahn 1970:5–6; Steiner 1968:260). Despite the creation of IRA tribal governments in the 1930s, the BIA's massive colonial-style bureaucratic administration remained in place. Local
non-Indian farmers were more likely to contact the agency superintendent than they were the tribal government to discuss issues involving

leasing, tribal property, or other relationships between the reservation and local non-Indian communities (Thomas 1967:39). BIA agents continued to play a dominant role in Lakota farming operations into the 1930s and 1940s. The experience of a man from Kyle speaks to the economic power of the BIA agents during that time: "In the long run the agent was pretty particular. My dad had a farm loan, but I never got one. To take it out you had to be married and go through some paperwork, so I kept working and then I got married, but it still wasn't enough for the agent to help me get started. So our neighbor paid me five dollars a week to feed his cows and all."

Nonagricultural Wage Labor

Like the terrain of the global economy, the local economies surrounding the reservations can be mapped based on the various types of work in which women and men of different races engage (Ward 1993:60). From the beginning of Pine Ridge and Rosebud, there has been differential access to wage work depending on the race of the applicant.

The BIA Agency was among the earliest sources for Lakota wage labor positions, but not all positions were open to Lakota workers. In the early reservation years, the agencies tried to be as self-sufficient as possible, employing Lakota men and women as clerks, butchers, laborers, watchmen, cooks, and housekeepers. The Lakota wage laborers invariably had to work under the supervision of non-Indian employees (FARC Pine Ridge 32-2, 1904–1914). In wage work settings, the concept of Lakota "need" was often used by the government to justify differential treatment of Indian and non-Indian employees. For example, in 1917 in Rosebud, the BIA employed two non-Indian regular salaried employees at $1,260 per year and thirty-five Indian irregular wage employees at $600 per year to manage and run the school farms, presumably reasoning that the Indians "needed" less to live on (FARC Rosebud A-436, 8/23/17:20).

As soon as reservations were created, the BIA agents helped manage and regulate the flow of Indian labor into the surrounding regional economy. The political context of the reservations at that time required that the BIA Indian agent grant permission for Lakotas to leave the reservation boundaries. There were a few job opportunities away from the highly regulated reservation. As early as the 1890s, Lakota men and their families were entering labor contracts with Buffalo Bill's and Will Penny's wild west shows and spending the spring and summer months traveling from North Platte, Nebraska, to the European continent (FARC Pine B-162–047, 1924; Moses 1995). Freedom from the oppressive hand of the agent was one factor among many that made this type of wage work opportunity attractive to Lakotas and distasteful to Indian agents. Rosebud Indian Agent Edward Kelly reflects this perspective in his letter of January 30, 1908, to the commissioner of Indian Affairs denying a request for Lakotas to participate in a wild west show: "My opinion is that Indians should either remain at home and look after their allotments and stock, or if they be allowed to go off the reserve that work be secured for them involving manual labor. I do not think that show life is the proper thing to teach them that they must work for a living. I am fully aware that very many Indians enjoy show life and they are always willing and anxious to go, but I do not think that it is the best thing for them to do" (FARC Rosebud B-162–047–181908, 1908).

In the handful of industrial projects that have been initiated on the reservations over the past century, the plant managers tend to be white and the supervisors and line workers Indian. The situation at the electronics plant in Manderson in 1977 was typical of Lakotas' experiences with industrialization. A former worker at the factory recalls: "I think people started boycotting the plant because of the low wages and no raises, and then the place burnt down and they never bothered bringing it back. There were Indian supervisors at the plant, but I think the manager was white."

In the contemporary South Dakota economy, the experiences and opportunities of non-Indians in and around the reservations in getting wage work are different from those of Indians. Unemployment in Pine Ridge in 1992 was 32.7 percent, but the unemployment rate for all of South Dakota was just 3 percent, and 7.5 percent for the United States as a whole. Of all the people in South Dakota who were unemployed in 1992, 88 percent of them were "nonwhite," with American Indians constituting the vast majority of "nonwhites" in the state (South Dakota Department of Labor 1992).

The imposition of a negative social identity ultimately restricts Lakotas to limited wage work opportunities on their reservations or confines them to the lower rungs of the socioeconomic ladder when they do venture beyond the reservation. Within the reservation region, many Lakota residents regard racism as the defining theme of interaction between Lakota and non-Indian communities in border towns.

Lakota consumers often receive mixed treatment in border towns and regional cities, being watched closely or physically accompanied by a white store clerk, for example, whereas non-Indians are free to shop and browse at their own pace. During the earliest days of reservation life, unscrupulous merchants were known to cheat Indian customers paying with cash, so some Lakota laborers preferred to be paid in food and other supplies (Cash & Hoover 1971:70; Paine 1935:64).

Border towns are often a necessary evil when Lakotas are looking for work, however. Several women told me about their experiences as children living and going to school in border towns where their fathers were working. One woman from Oglala shares her memories: "My dad worked for the Burlington, for the train, over there in Chadron, so that's where we grew up, over there in Nebraska. There was a lot of prejudice. I remember because I used to fight for my sisters and me because they'd call us squaws. I said, 'I'm an Indian, but I'm not a squaw,' and then they'd call me squaw again and first thing you know I'm fighting her. There weren't very much Lakota people there then, not like there is now. Just some rail workers." Another woman from Potato Creek tells about her experience while her father worked in Scottsbluff, Nebraska:

> The white kids they really making fun of us, in the bus they don't want us to sit close to them. So there was three of us, so we sit close together, we sit in one seat. And the white kids are all hiding up at the counter because they don't want to come close to us. One boy, he sit beside us or in front of us or behind us, he got red hair and freckle face, and pretty soon he got into an argument with them. They said that we're poor and sick and dirty and everything, you know, and he say, "Yeah, maybe you're right but look around, this is their land, you guys took over their land, and they got gold and you guys took over," things like that, and he got in a fight with one boy, so he got suspended from the bus. After that, his parents took him back and forth, so we have a rough time in the bus. Pretty soon I just couldn't take it, so I stopped. That's how I didn't go to school.

One outspoken community leader in Pine Ridge describes a local border town as the "asshole of the world" for its discriminatory treatment of Indian people.

Even in the regional cities, racism is an issue. An elderly woman from the Rosebud Reservation remembers looking for off-reservation work in the mid-1900s: "We left the reservation in 1940 to look for higher wages. I got a fellowship to go to college, but it was only enough for one semester, so then I worked to become an LPN through a work training program. First we lived down in Nebraska, then we moved up to Rapid [City], but it was really rough. No one would rent to us because we were Indian, so we had to live in a cabin to start with, and it was terrible, so small our feet were practically hanging out. This motel owner we stayed near, he took a liking to us and finally arranged for a place for us to rent."

A constant source of contention and frustration within the reservation communities is the tremendous amount of money that is lost to the

Lakota economy because it is spent in non-Indian stores in border towns and regional cities. According to a businessman from St. Francis: "The reservation is not a poverty area. One project estimated that between Pine Ridge and Rosebud, there is about $800 million generated and spent annually, including government programs. So the prosperity of the non-Indian border towns as well as Rapid City and Pierre turns on this financing. There is no multiplier effect for the reservation economies."

As the distance from the reservation increases, the social identity of Indians improves for those Lakota people with the skills and training to be part of the middle—and upper—class (A. Kehoe 1989:57). They are often induced off the reservation to urban areas, where the politics of identity, though still present, is less confining. As one local Lakota small business person in Rosebud notes, "I can't afford Indians who are well qualified in computer work, because I have to compete with the big corporations in the West who want to have an Indian on staff."

The administration of Indians has been a major source of employment for non-Indians since the creation of reservations. In the decades of effort to improve economic conditions on Pine Ridge and Rosebud, non-Indians have dominated the payrolls of the schools, churches, hospitals, social services, and state courts that exist to meet the needs of a nearly exclusive Lakota clientele.

One common complaint is that non-Indian employees on the reservations need to be more sensitive to the Lakota community they ostensibly serve. Although most of the BIA office workers are Indian, teachers in the BIA schools and doctors and health-care workers at the Indian Health Service are largely non-Indian employees willing to relocate to Rosebud or Pine Ridge for months or years. A community activist from Rosebud argues: "We need to organize a screening and orientation for the hiring of BIA school workers and IHS hospital workers. They are coming to the reservation to redo the Indian, and they can't or don't want to understand what's going on. The community gets fed up with that attitude. Some training and workshops for people coming to this area on identifying racism would be a good start."

Lakota workers are most often deemed unqualified for positions because of their level of educational achievement. The social identity of Indians as incapable, uneducated, and inferior continues in some ways to be enforced and reproduced through the public education system in South Dakota. The BIA operates day schools in most of the districts and a boarding school in Pine Ridge Village. The state of South Dakota operates five county schools on the Pine Ridge Reservation and three county schools on Rosebud. The county schools have a higher percentage of non-

Indian students from rural areas and incorporated towns who are not eligible for BIA schools. Although the BIA schools are slightly more willing
to address concerns about student needs or to integrate Lakota culture
into the curriculum, both have predominantly non-Indian teachers and
administrators. The county schools are less likely than the BIA schools to
offer Lakota language or culture courses, even though the vast majority
of their students are Lakotas.

The school system has long been identified as an important institution
controlled by the dominant culture to disseminate mainstream cultural
views to minority youth (Bailey and Flores 1973:192–94). That perspective is supported by the educational system in Pine Ridge and Rosebud,
which is seen by some Lakotas as racist and conservative. According to a
woman from St. Francis:

> There is a lot of racism within the schools here. It is hard to understand
> why anyone would come here to teach and not be motivated to work with
> Indian children. I guess a lot of them are the relatives of ranchers and they
> can't overcome the attitudes they were raised with, but it is really upsetting.
> And many stay in the school system who have become so negative and so
> cynical that they can't think of any improvements. They just put up bar-
> riers to any new ideas. It's hard too because the parents are still not taking
> a role in what the schools are doing. It is like the respect they show for
> others is not returned, and they won't confront others about their racism
> or their closed minds, so it ends up being the children who suffer.

Others identify deliberate attempts to keep Lakota parents from being
active in school life. A Lakota mother from Spring Creek describes her
feelings about the local school system: "Teachers make parents feel like
they have to leave the kids at the door, and everything beyond that door
is not the parents' business. It's a real contrast to Head Start, where you
are encouraged to be involved and have a voice in the education of your
child. By the time they get to public school, they make you feel uncomfortable even going into the school or asking about what the teacher is
presenting to your kids. There are teachers that have no business being
there at all, because they are racists and can't get beyond their own limitations so they put the low feeling and self-hatred onto our kids."

Because of concerns over racism in the schools, there is a growing
motivation to train Lakotas to replace non-Indian teachers and administrators; such personnel would have both the technical training and the
cultural sensitivity to do a better job for the community. It is strongly
believed on the reservation that Lakota teachers provide a better educational experience for Lakota students.

Some of the most painful reservation conflicts arise over schools that are operated by the state but attended by a majority of Lakota students. Lakota parents face the prospect of being required by law to send their children to educational institutions that in substance and attitude are derogatory to their Indian identity. On Rosebud, the problem of the county schools' treatment of Lakota culture, language, and history became acute in 1991 as the school board elections approached and people again confronted the fact that a school system with more than 80 percent Lakota students had only one Lakota member on its school board. To discuss and deal with this problem, a series of meetings was held under the title Task Force Against Racism. A young woman from Rosebud summarizes the conflict: "There is resistance on the School Board of Todd County to integrating Lakota studies and language into the basic school curriculum. The process of school board restructuring has involved all kinds of racism. The Voting Rights Act looks at outcome, not intent, so if we don't retain an Indian majority on the board, I think we should sue." Despite these efforts to organize the community, inadequate Lakota representation on the school board continues to be a problem.

The advent of the Indian Self-Determination and Education Act of 1975, mentioned earlier, improved the hiring of Indians in federal government positions (Stubben 1994:111). The 1970s brought the first major change in local economic relations. But this improvement is not without its debits. As an Indian Health Service worker in Rosebud reports: "There is a catch to the BIA or IHS Indian Preference provisions in that, if an Indian person comes in, then they automatically are put in under the preference, and they have to wait three years before their step promotion kicks in, whereas if a white person comes in, they only have to wait one year, regardless if they are more or less qualified than the Indian who started at the same time." Furthermore, because of the political economy of qualification, a wide range of government positions are still predominantly staffed by non-Indians. Although administrators, clerical workers, cooks, bus drivers, and maintenance workers tend to be Lakota, many professional-level positions, such as professors, doctors, and teachers, are held by non-Indians. More and more Lakota young people are getting the training needed for these positions, but it is a gradual process. When a young woman from Rosebud graduated from medical school recently, there was a full-length article about her in the newspaper *Indian Country Today*.

Small Business

Lakotas interested in operating small businesses also encounter varying degrees of resistance to crossing racially defined class lines developed over the last century. Many small businesses depend on government programs, such as road construction projects, implemented by private contractors who hire workers for the term of the contract. The general perception by Lakotas is that non-Indians get these lucrative government contracts whereas Indians receive the temporary menial jobs to perform the work required by the contracts. A woman from Pine Ridge asserts: "You know with the government, there are white contractors that buy them from the Indian people who front for them. Like all that BIA, IHS, Housing Authority money, that should all be Indian preference and we should have Indian people ready with their small businesses to take up every single one of those contracts, rather than the white contractors."

The Tribal Employment and Contract Rights Office in Rosebud (TECRO) and the Tribal Employment Rights Office in Pine Ridge (TERO) were established to ensure that tribal members receive jobs whenever contractors perform services for the tribe or the federal government within the reservation. However, the bulk of the jobs that these programs have been able to secure for tribal members are entry-level, minimum-wage, and limited-skills positions. Virtually all the upper management positions are held by off-reservation non-Indians. In 1992, for example, the TECRO Job Skills Bank had close to a thousand short-term positions for "laborers" but fewer than one hundred for heavy equipment operators and none for managerial roles. As a result, little training and mentoring for future Lakota contractors actually takes place. A woman with TERO notes: "There are only nine Lakota subcontractors on the rez right now. Financial resources is the main thing holding them back. I knew a guy who couldn't get a contract just because of a $750 insurance requirement. No one around here is willing to insure Indian people. I see it every day, the bad treatment they get from non-Indian prime contractors. Non-Indian contractors are getting $125-plus each week just to drive to work, but the Indian employees aren't getting it." One Indian construction manager confided to me that winning construction contracts depends on how racist the prime contractor is reputed to be.

Lakota small businesses also face more of a challenge when reaching out to non-Indian business customers. A Lakota businessman from the Pine Ridge Reservation recalls the emotional and financial stress of encountering racism and rejection from non-Indian customers:

> I packed up some cases and went around to different stores, didn't know nothing about marketing or being a salesman. I still think the product sells itself. Some said they'd try, others said, "Get out of here." After a while, I'd sit in the motel and say, "Don't take it personal." That was the hard part. Every store I have a family history on the store owner and what they like,

so I can small talk and get to know them, so they identify my product with me and they'll invest time in my product. But it's hard to take the rejection. I don't think there should be any distinctions made because of your color, it shouldn't make a difference, and a person can make it whether they're Indian or white in business. Sometimes it's harder, you have to go that extra mile to get their respect, but you have to be professional and keep your business attractive to the people who use your product.

Because of difficulties reaching white consumers, a wider network of tribes and tribal members around the country has become the main customer base for many of the Lakotas' small businesses. One Rosebud businessman explains: "I work with a tribal member in Minnesota, who got a contract for work with a computer company." Another businessman from Antelope describes his client strategy: "If I do work for one specific office, like if I got a contract to computerize the courthouse, and get them happy with the system, then there are six other tribes in the area that want the same done for them. I've worked with tribes in Oklahoma, in the Northwest, North Dakota. I've worked with a lot of people."

For the reservation economies as a whole, when the dimension of race is placed into the equation, it is possible to see that the flow of economic opportunities of the world economy is diverted based on the race of the participant. In all the formal, market-based economic activities such as wage work, commodity agriculture, and small business, the social identity of race works to delimit those areas that are open to Lakota people and those areas that are closed. Economic opportunities are controlled not only in the direct search for jobs, credit, and customers but in the indirect pursuits of education, housing, and interpersonal respect.

Social Identity and the Special Problem of Alcohol

The economic impact of social identity goes beyond the direct issue of differential access to land, capital, wage work, and business opportunities, or even the indirect issue of differential treatment by the dominant society. Social identity affects an individual's self-conception of just what economic activities are within reach. Alcoholism can be used as a lens for tracing the economic effects of negative social identity on Lakota individuals and households.

Of all the strains on reservation communities, the issue of alcohol is among the most recurring and most intractable (Beauvais 1998; Bucko 1998:91, 174–75; Graves 1971; Medicine 1983b). Of the one hundred people I formally interviewed, 68 percent reported either having personally endured a period of alcoholism or having a close relative with a serious alcohol problem. Interestingly enough, between 1989 and 1992, the Strong Heart Study determined that 47.4 percent of the population of Cheyenne River, Devil's Lake, and Oglala Sioux between the ages of forty-five and seventy-five were current users of alcohol, compared with the national statistic of 57 percent of the adult population using alcohol in 1985 (May 1996:239). The problem seems to rest on the difference between alcohol use and abuse. Alcohol abuse is not limited to any economic class or social segment of the reservation communities. Tribal councilmen and construction workers alike are reported to be drinkers. As Lakotas confront and debate their options in today's world, they are reconsidering the place of alcohol, particularly its role in suppressing Lakota identity. Sobriety is increasingly being regarded by Lakotas as an assertion of their identity.

The issue of alcoholism is discussed openly and frequently in all contexts of reservation life. Individuals struggling with alcohol are certainly not invisible. Many community and development leaders went through periods of alcohol abuse in their twenties and thirties (see May 1996:242). "Drugs and alcohol don't belong to the Lakota people," a Kyle man explains. "I used it for about six years when I was twenty-one years old, because I married and I thought I was a man so I should use alcohol. But I finally realized it was no good." Vietnam-era veterans report problems with alcohol. Lakotas offer many explanations for the high incidence of alcoholism.

Alcoholic relatives present special challenges for Lakota conceptions of obligations to family. Alcoholic relatives represent a drain on limited household resources, in terms of money spent for alcohol, lost hours of productivity, emotional disruption, and negative encounters with the legal system (Red Shirt 1998:42–45). An attorney from Antelope notes that it is not uncommon for intoxicated individuals, some of them extended family, to come by his house at eleven o'clock at night or later to ask for money, seek legal help to recover custody of a child or to file suit for a past grievance, or call and ask to be bailed out of jail: "It took me a long time to figure out how to deal with people when they've been drinking. I used to try to deal with them, but I got to the point where now I just tell them to go home and come back when they're sober, that I'll still love them when they sober up, but while they're drunk they are not a lovable person."

The impact of drinking on Lakota young people is particularly poignant. The community struggles over a difficult balance between the Lakota belief that children are innocent and should not be punished and the mainstream belief that strict discipline is needed to deal with increas-

ing incidences of violence, drug and alcohol abuse, and teenage preg-
nancy among Lakota young people. According to a Kyle man, "I'd say for
drugs and alcohol, only about 2 to 3 percent of the young people are into
that. The rest are thinking about the future, how to better themselves and
their community, to be proud of themselves." Some felt the problems of
Lakota youth are due to the example their parents are setting, particularly parents with drinking problems. Lakotas often correlate drinking
with a breakdown in the traditional ideals of adult responsibility toward
children.

A common practice is to have children of alcoholic parents live with
their grandparents or other relatives. A woman from Wanbli recalls: "My
parents were into alcohol, so I don't remember them ever really working steady at any jobs. I don't know how they got along. I was raised
by my grandparents." One Kyle woman's family situation is typical: "My
nephew's mom took him back for a while, but there was drinking going
on in her household, so he called me up and I went and got him. I thought
it was good that he felt he could call me like that, and that he didn't have
to be in that kind of an environment, that there was an alternative that he
preferred." A woman from St. Francis attributes the breakdown in family
values and family structure to the prevalence of alcoholism: "It goes along
with all the drinking and alcoholism, it ends up being the children who
suffer, and the children are suffering." Lakota children of alcoholics with
no relatives to take them in may become foster children. A woman from
Wanbli was separated not only from her alcoholic parents but also from
her siblings because her foster parents were able to take only a single child
into their household. Her foster parents were non-Indian, adding more
issues of social identity and self-esteem to her already full plate.

Alcohol can provide a consistent motivation for economic activity.
One Kyle woman recovering from alcoholism remembers her drinking
days when she and her husband spent all their time raising money for
"The Cause." A segment of the Lakota population engages in temporary
odd jobs just to earn money to buy alcohol. As one elderly St. Francis
man recalls of his youth: "I did odd jobs to make money for drinking. I'd
hitch rides from town to town, and some white guy would approach me.
'You want to make money?' So I unloaded freight cars filled with cement
blocks." Local men with drinking problems can at times provide a cheap
source of labor, albeit an unreliable one.

Drinking is most evident at the beginning of each month, when paychecks, BIA General Assistance checks, Social Security checks, and TANF
checks are issued. Those with drinking problems are also motivated to
find methods of exchanging their Food Stamps, which may not be used to

purchase alcohol or tobacco. Microenterprise was often used as a method for raising quick cash for alcohol, leading to the problems of both low quality and low prices, which hurt the market for serious microenterprise producers. One woman described buying some *thípsila* braid. "This guy kind of drinks a lot and uses the money for that." At the end of the month, craft producers with drinking problems sell items cheaply to continue their access to alcohol until the new checks come through. As a result, one Potato Creek woman says sternly: "I won't teach quill work to drinkers."

Alcohol plays a major role in the economic relationships between the residents of Pine Ridge and the reservation border towns. On the one hand, border towns find it lucrative to feed the addiction of alcoholic tribal members. One border town bar was known for its willingness to buy Food Stamps so people could drink. White Clay, Nebraska, two miles south of the Pine Ridge Reservation with a population of twenty-two, accounted for more than 80 percent of the sales of alcohol in its county of Sheridan in 1997, with more than 90 percent of its customers coming from the Pine Ridge Reservation (*Indian Country Today* 7/5-12/99, B4). The four liquor stores in White Clay are reported to have sales totaling millions of dollars each year (*Indian Country Today* 7/26–8/2/99, B2; Frazier 1999:72).

On the other hand, non-Indian border town residents use alcoholism as a basis for condemning Indian people and discounting their rights to justice and fair treatment. As a student from Red Cloud Indian School wrote, "The people who work at the White Clay bars complain about the Indians lying around by their bar or sitting around drinking. They recognize the problem and yet they are part of the problem. They sell the beer which makes the Indians stick around the bars" (*Indian Country Today* 10/11–18/99, A4).

A particularly tragic example of the unintended incentives created by public assistance occurred when ssi disability benefits were extended to the condition known as fetal alcohol syndrome (FAS). Stories began circulating of Lakota women, already struggling with alcoholism, being encouraged to continue drinking for the additional benefits a child with FAS would receive. "FAS is fairly new," a Kyle woman explains, "maybe twenty years at the longest, and now it's at the point where, well, for a while they were saying they'd get more money if their babies had FAS because they'd get ssi, and I thought that was really sad, because a lot of them were not really caring, because they'd still get help, and even more help than if they were just on welfare." The Rosebud Tribe took a hand at creating its own incentives against drinking, making it a crime for a pregnant woman to drink alcohol. Many community members found the prospect of criminalizing women who needed treatment and counseling equally unfortunate.

The abuse of alcohol is often a great topic of concern in the Lakota workplace, affecting productivity and the mental environment. The situation of a Rosebud woman is all too common:

> You really can't expect total job satisfaction. But like at my office, one woman struggles to get through the week and then drinks on weekends, and the other woman I work with has a serious drug problem, so all around it affects me. They come to work grouchy and they can't handle the stress of the job. The leadership at the office, he thinks he's doing a good job, but some days he just isn't functioning. And I'm about the only one in that office that stood up to him when he's taking everything out on the office staff. They have an employee alcohol program, so I feel like going to the director, but even the EAP [Employee Assistance Program] workshop I went to in Rapid [City], my coworker was out partying the whole night before. I really like my job, but I get tired of this and want to quit. I feel like I'm caught in a bad place. A lot of that goes on with the tribe, and on the community level, if you get a little healthy and then it's all around you.

The impact of alcohol on working seems to be increasing. Many Lakotas spot a contrast in the relationship between working and drinking among the older generation. One Kyle man in his sixties observes: "Most of my age group that I knew at the ranch and at school, alcohol took them away. In the old days, people would drink, but they'd quit and go do what they were doing the next day. Now they just keep drinking and don't do anything else." A Wanbli woman in her forties recalls: "My dad was an alcoholic too, but he still provided for the family, for him it never came to a choice between the family and being drunk. But my ex-husband crossed that line and couldn't even provide for himself."

The use of alcohol and drugs by tribal representatives is another troubling issue. One tribal employee told me:

> Sobriety is a real issue for the ethics, judgment, and ability of the tribal council to represent the tribe, since most of them are either bingers or constant drunks. Some aren't, some are recovering. But one, for example, has been on a binge for two months. And yet Finance calls him over to get his travel check. He'll really be a good representative for the tribe in that condition [sarcastically]. Even if you give him coffee, he'll just be an alert drunk. Seems like there should be some fiduciary duty on Finance not to give out checks when they're in that kind of condition. They passed that resolution in 1990 to achieve sobriety for the reservation by the year 2000, and they haven't done anything to implement it. If the council won't confront its own drinking, how can they provide leadership? And the people

keep electing these drunks because the communities haven't confronted
their own drinking, so they don't see it as a problem.

Lakotas who attend meetings of national Indian organizations have returned with stories of how tribal council members embarrass them and
the tribe by skipping sessions to go drinking or appearing at sessions
under the influence of alcohol and drugs. "They knew they had to show
up for the closing session," one person confided, "or the word would get
back home that they missed all the purposes for being at the conference."

The conflicted role of Christianity, its imposition on Lakota people as
part of the process of economic and political incorporation, and its impact on Lakota social identity are sometimes connected to the problem of
alcoholism. Some Lakotas see Christianity as a form of emotional support
that helps Lakota people overcome addiction to alcohol. Many recovering alcoholics attribute their ability to change their lives and leave alcohol
behind to their faith in Jesus and the support of the church congregation.

Other Lakotas share the blunt opinion of a St. Francis woman: "I
see some of the problems we are having with alcohol and the failure to
reach out to those people with alcohol problems as being the fault of
the church." These problems often revolve around intergenerational religious tensions. Some younger Lakotas are disillusioned with the decisions
the older generation made and the impact of those decisions on their
community and the tribe. Their main complaint centers on the adoption
of non-Indian practices and beliefs at the expense of Lakota traditions:
"This cousin of mine, he's really into Lakota spirituality and is a medicine
man, and he said one day that we should just throw all those Catholics
and Episcopals and Christians off the reservation and really let the healing process start. But I told him you'd have a problem with the little old
ladies here who are really into the church, and he said, 'Well, go ahead
and throw them out too,' but I said you'd have a big fight on your hands
then [laughs]." Elders whom outside anthropologists would deem the
most authentically Lakota are often the most devoutly Christian, whereas
younger people are often more conscious of Lakota spiritual concepts
and practices because they are actively seeking to revive them. As one
Antelope woman working to combat alcoholism in her community explains: "My mom still pressures me to follow Christianity and questions
my involvement in sweats and my interest in Lakota religion. I wish she
could see why I have such problems with the church." A Rosebud man
who had overcome an alcohol problem respected his mother's faith and
commitment to the local mission but at the same time had nothing but
anger for his own physical and emotional abuse at the mission boarding
school.

The Rosebud and Pine Ridge Reservations have taken different approaches to the criminalization of alcohol consumption and alcoholism. In Pine Ridge, the sale and possession of alcohol is a criminal offense under the tribal code, but it is legal in Rosebud. In Pine Ridge, the perception was "over at Rosebud that they do lots of drinking, because you can buy it right there on the rez." A Manderson man asserts: "I think they should keep alcohol illegal on the rez. I think they should close the borders of the rez and put way stations with a pole at each of the entrances, and then they could search the cars for alcohol and drugs. They can't stop people from drinking, but they could make them leave the rez to do it."

Bootleggers and drug dealers are another fairly invisible but regularly discussed component of the reservation economy. The specter of bootleggers is still present on the Pine Ridge Reservation, where the sale of alcohol continues to be illegal. Those opposed to alcohol on the Pine Ridge Reservation note with disgust that bootleggers are never caught. "Some have been bootlegging so good so that they never get caught," a Pine Ridge man explains. "They'll be in and out of the business in two months, so they don't get caught at it, or they pass the kitty along so no one can trace it to them." Bootleggers are not new to the reservation economy. "My grandfather was a bootlegger," a man from Rosebud told me. "He was disabled, so that was the way he made his living. That was back when they had class and ethics."

Alcohol was also associated with other forms of criminal activity. Drinking is often a factor in brawls and break-ins in the cluster housing units, as a former resident confirms: "The housing there in Kyle is really bad. They even broke the door in, the kids there were really bad, the neighbor's kids kept breaking in my back door. There were people fighting with a gun, drunken, and broke in my window during this chasing with guns, and no one around there would help out or anything, so I was glad to move away from there." Stolen items are sold or hocked to pay for alcohol. A Rosebud woman reports the heavy impact of these burglaries: "At my mom's house, they took her beadwork, stole that and some star quilts too, they stole it and sold it. So she wants to call the Housing and have them moved out of there. People around here will steal things. This guy who lives in the elderly apartments and beads, somebody got in through his window and stole all his things."

The common association between alcohol and violence led to racially divided interpretations of the political conflicts in White Clay during the summer of 1999. From the Lakota perspective, the protests were aimed at long-term civil rights and justice issues raised by the deaths of Wilson Black Elk Jr. and Ronald Hard Heart, whose bodies were found in

White Clay on June 8 (*Indian Country Today* 7/12–19/99, A1). Rumors circulated on the reservation that the Sheridan County sheriff's office was
not investigating these and other murders of Indian people in the same
fashion as non-Indian murders and that police brutality played a role in
their deaths. Black Elk's niece reported that he had a ninety-dollar unpaid
bar tab in White Clay. "Black Elk appeared frightened and told her the
bar owner said he would have 'the sheriff or his boys handle it' " (*Indian
Country Today* 7/12–19/99, A3). The local non-Indian press emphasized
the violence sparked by the protests and the property damage suffered by
the White Clay business owners (*Gillette News-Record* 6/27/99, A1), but
mentioned the unsolved slayings only in passing and without reference
to the sheriff's office (*Gillette News-Record* 6/27/99, A12).

Alcohol is also a recurring factor in the growing numbers of car accidents and suicides on the reservations. Car accidents take a disproportionate toll on the lives of reservation residents, through a combination
of older cars, tremendous distances to travel, poor road conditions, and
the constant danger of drunken driving (Young 1996:63–64, 68). On one
particularly unsettling drive, the two women riding with me were able to
identify the crash sites of more than a dozen extended family members
between Oglala and Rapid City. Another woman lost her only two sons in
separate car accidents less than a year apart. Suicide is another drinking-
related tragedy disproportionately prevalent on the reservations, particularly among teenagers (Young 1996:60). "My youngest sister killed herself at age nineteen, in a drinking incident when she was at a low point
of a long depression, so it took me years to get over that loss and come
to grips with her own decision. So that's why for now my kids come first,
and the kids they hang out with too. They all know they can come by
our place and have a safe environment, and that you can have a good
time that doesn't involve drinking." A greater susceptibility to AIDS has
also been linked to the problem of alcoholism in American Indian communities, where alcohol abuse lowers the immune system response and
reduced inhibitions lead to unprotected sex (Vernon 1997).

Heightened awareness about the effects of alcoholism has created a
bifurcation between drinkers and nondrinkers, with no middle ground.
One woman noted that at her family reunion, no one in the family drinks
casually anymore, even though none had been alcoholics before. Board
members of one non-governmental organization debated having complete sobriety as a qualification to serve on the board, to the exclusion of
anyone who had even an occasional drink. If anyone kept wine or beer
in the refrigerator, the immediate assumption was that it would be used

to get drunk. One woman in a child custody battle was accused of being a drinker because she had a glass of champagne on New Year's Eve.

Some Lakotas feel there is more alcohol abuse now than when they were younger. An elder man from Kyle agrees: "The last ten years, alcohol and especially drugs have been bad. Before that it was just alcohol, and twenty years ago it wasn't that bad." A woman from Rosebud notes with disgust: "There are some young people who are homeless and live in the elderly housing, but they're homeless because of alcohol. Instead of paying their money to HUD, they drink it up or smoke marijuana, and then they can't pay their bills, so they get kicked out. They could be like everyone else if they'd just stop drinking." Some, like one woman from Pine Ridge, attributes the rise in drinking to the generation currently in middle age: "Now the elderly are dying, more of them each year, but the generation in the middle isn't coming up into the same things. They're really into drinking now in the community, and they don't do anything else. There aren't even enough softball teams to do tournaments anymore." A woman from Wanbli observes a shift in gender and alcohol: "I think the drinking is more now than when I was a girl. Like my dad would drink, but not my mom. And it didn't interfere with anything. Now the women drink too, and that's bad. Like my niece, she'll come over here all sad and crying, and I tell her, 'Stop with the drinking and the drugs, and then you'll be all right again.'"

Others feel the situation with alcohol is improving now that recovery and sobriety are a prominent part of the public discourse on the reservations. "Alcohol is a big thing that really pulls them down," a woman from Kyle acknowledges. "I think alcohol was really, really bad and it's getting better now, by educating them and having it in the school programs and having it in all of our programs." A woman from Rosebud shares her perspective on how those struggling for sobriety are received by the community:

> I know a lot of people who were, I'd say that they were recovered, they don't call themselves recovered, they have this thing about saying, always saying that they're recovering, even though they've been sober for twenty years. But I know a lot of people that had been alcoholic and who admitted they were alcoholics, and are sober now, and are a real strong force in the community, who have a lot to say about what goes on. Having been through that struggle, I guess they're stronger for it. They're not hiding anymore. It used to be that if you were an alcoholic it was shameful and you didn't talk about it and nobody was supposed to know. But now everybody's willing to say, "Oh yeah, I used to drink," and "I've been sober three years" or whatever it is, and they are allowed to be part of the community.

I just think that's wonderful, that we're not wasting these people, because so many of us have problems with alcohol, if we're going to do that, throw away everybody who's ever had a drinking problem, well, you're looking at three-fourths of our community.

Alcoholism has taken a toll on virtually every aspect of reservation life in Pine Ridge and Rosebud. The economic drain caused by alcoholism only increases the poverty created by the economic and political incorporation of the Lakotas into the world system. Ultimately, as the community takes the initiative in creating new treatment approaches that acknowledge the damage done to Lakota cultural identity by the incorporation process, "the sacred hoop will be mended."

6
The Political Economy of Need

It is common for academics to debate what government social and economic policies would better meet the needs of the poor. What constitutes a "need" is not self-evident or culturally neutral, however. Worldwide, what indigenous people determine they need has not necessarily been what the beneficiaries of the world system have wanted them to need.

The interpretation of needs is itself a politically contested arena. This political contest takes place over whether to recognize a need as legitimate, over how to define what would satisfy that need, and finally over whether to satisfy it (Fraser 1989:144–58; H. Moore 1992:36–37, 141; Schmink 1984:91). At each juncture, there are competing concepts of need as defined by local cultures and traditions on the one hand and by the culture and expectations of the world economy on the other hand. The world economy has great power to homogenize and "naturalize" needs that in reality further the interests of capital, sometimes to the detriment of a local culture whose "needs" are supposedly being met (Castile and Bee 1992:6).

Three broad areas of need are explored here that are critical to indigenous people in general and to the Lakotas in particular: the need for self-governance, the need for economic development, and the need for support to prevent households from falling below a minimal standard of living. I argue that tremendous efforts and resources are spent on Pine Ridge and Rosebud to meet needs, but not those needs defined by the Lakotas.

Need for Self-Governance

One of the concepts behind self-government is the prospect of institutions that will be responsive to the needs of the local citizenry. The assumption for reservations is that when tribal institutions are involved, the needs of the people, as they define them, will be met. The tribal government is the main point of contact for many of the essential federal programs mediating economic gaps for local residents. At the same time, the responsiveness of these tribal bureaucracies to their members continues to be constrained by extensive federal regulation and financial control. The history of the current institutions defined as representing the Lakota people raises the question whether the local cultural definitions of need are the ones satisfied by tribal government. As a result, an understandable degree of tension and frustration exists for both the tribal employees and the tribal members who encounter this bureaucracy.

The Re-Creation of Tribal Government

The creation of reservation boundaries in the late nineteenth century and the recognition of Western-style tribal governments by the United States in the 1930s are critical components in the incorporation of the Lakotas into the capitalist world economy. The emergence of the capitalist world economy entailed the development of nation-states throughout the world that, in turn, participate in but do not control the international economic system. No zone has been allowed to exist without becoming part of some particular nation, and consequently no individual or group can escape the authority of some nation (Wallerstein 1991:189–90).

In the historic formation of the territory that is now defined as the United States, independent American Indian groups were conducting their activities outside the sphere of control of any external state structure and were not themselves organized as sovereign nation-states. By concluding treaties with these tribes, the United States not only defined territorial boundaries but, perhaps more important, created sovereign native states that were treated, at least ideologically, as legally equal to any other nation-state. As the treaty process was gradually transformed into the process of creating reservations, the terminology of sovereign nations was used to create the notion of tribes as geographically bounded domestic dependent nations. Tribal governments, as the official representatives of these sovereign nations, were propelled into the world economy, contributing significant flows of land and minerals, migratory labor, and capital from the consumption of consumer goods to the dominant sectors of the U.S. economy.

Traditional Lakota tribal leadership was challenged and manipulated as the Lakotas were integrated into the world system (Fenelon 1998:147–49, 153–54). Lakota men who were willing to cooperate with U.S. treaty objectives were often elevated to the status of "treaty chiefs" by the United States, regardless of their actual standing within their communities, and given special access by the United States to goods and decision-making power (Biolsi 1992:37–38). Once the Lakotas were confined to reservations, there was a forced deterioration of the traditional political system. Initially, BIA agents exercised total authoritarian control over the reservation and the people (Black Hills State College 1975:9). The BIA agency superintendent used rations, which had become the main source of food on the reservations, as a weapon to challenge and weaken the authority of the *tiyóšpaye* leaders. Although preexisting leaders were still recognized within their *tiyóšpaye*, new leaders with more power were appointed by the BIA agents and given authority over the distribution of critical annuities and rations (Holder 1970:111, 123, 129; Hyde 1937:34, 39, 56, 61–62, 65–67, 81–83, 308; Standing Bear 1928:71, 73; Walker 1982:24, 141). The federal government also attempted to strip contentious chiefs of their influence. Those who followed the path marked by the superintendent were labeled "progressive"; those who were rebellious and uncooperative with agency views were "conservative," "traditional," and "backward" (Biolsi 1992:xx–xxi; Cornell 1988:37; Hyde 1956:20–21; Hyde 1937:40, 67; Utley 1963:26–28; Walker 1982:149). Furthermore, the reservation, rather than the *tiyóšpaye* or the Lakota subdivision, became the central political unit (Cornell 1988:36). The subsequently created reservation tribal governments were new creations representing new entities (Biolsi 1992:4–5, 46–47; Canby 1983:55–56; Cornell 1988:36–37; Hoxie 1985:58–59, 61; Hurt 1987:65).

The Indian Reorganization Act, passed in 1934, promised to create genuine tribal self-government. The establishment of IRA tribal governments ostensibly acknowledged the need for Lakota self-governance, but the satisfaction of that need was interpreted through the perspective of the U.S. government. The federal government required that the Lakota tribal governments adhere to the U.S. version of a democratic institution. The BIA handed out to the tribes form constitutions and uniform tribal governments based on Euro-American democratic institutions, for the stated purpose of giving tribes self-governance (Biolsi 1992:98–99; Cornell 1988:36). The newly created Lakota tribal governments had the alien features of elections, terms of office, voting districts with no correspondence to any meaningful social unit, and delegation of representational power (Biolsi 1992:179). The externally oriented structures of the tribal government supported the federal government's conception of what was good for the tribe (Jorgensen 1971:70–71). Moreover, genuine tribal self-determination was blocked by structural limitations, as shown by the repeated references in tribal constitutions to approval of tribal council decisions by the secretary of the interior, just one blatant example of the federal government's continuing interference in tribal affairs (Cahn 1970: 22; Fay 1967:48; Parker 1975:53; Taylor 1980:95).

Prior U.S. policies of undermining and dismantling the social, political, and religious institutions of the Lakotas created a healthy skepticism among reservation residents toward this new policy of encouraging Lakota self-rule. Many identified the reservation tribal government simply as a puppet of the United States, the latest version of the "treaty chiefs" paraded before them. Others continued to view these externally created tribal governments not as political representatives but as people assigned to get as much as possible for Lakotas from the federal government. Still others saw tribal government as an avenue for developing and exercising the tribal sovereignty that had rightfully been the people's all along and was only now being recognized (Biolsi 1992:179; V. Deloria 1969:130–31; V. Deloria and Lytle 1984:197–98, 242; Walker 1982:149).

As a result, Lakotas today are extremely ambiguous about the tribal governments of Pine Ridge and Rosebud. On the one hand, the tribal government is the repository of all the remains of the sovereignty of Lakota people. Hence any expressions of disrespect toward the tribal government from local, state, or federal governments or from non-Indian businesses or individuals are regarded as an affront to Lakota sovereignty. Furthermore, through its jobs and programs, the tribal government represents a major redistributor of resources to individuals and families within the otherwise limited reservation economy.

On the other hand, the current configuration of tribal government is not a traditional Lakota institution but is itself a product of decades of federal government policies and actions. Lakotas continuously discuss and debate their concerns over the ethics, competence, and legitimacy of the tribal government. As a man from Kyle expresses it: "The structure of the tribal government is a wide subject, and you can't really answer a question about tribal government without stepping on somebody's toes, but there is definite room for improvement. It's not a viable government now."

Managing Contradictions

The myriad contradictions contained within the structure of the Lakota tribal governments lead to an overwhelming sense of paralysis. Because of the historic complexities and competing motives that created the context for tribal government, there are no obvious right answers or even black-and-white choices for those who take on the role of tribal politician. Fostering economic development can twist into undermining

Lakota cultural traditions; adopting Lakota approaches to governance can degrade into promoting nepotism, corruption, and incompetence; supporting public assistance programs can mean encouraging dependency among tribal members; resisting public assistance programs can result in abandoning the needs of the severely poor reservation residents. These contradictions are so apparent from the onset that it becomes difficult for those committed to tribal self-governance even to take a first step.

Tribal leaders are required to meet the standards of both Western government and Lakota government and often end up appearing dysfunctional under both systems. The tensions between competing and often incompatible demands lead to unusual extremes of behavior. Good leaders are noted for paying for the poor out of their own pockets. The receipt of small gifts by a political leader creates the obligation within the Lakota system to reciprocate with a favor. Within the Western system of government, direct favors for gifts are defined as corruption. Similarly, the motivation to help extended family members, required within the Lakota value system, would be roundly condemned as nepotism within the Western system.

Reservation communities also encounter major contradictions between the mainstream approach of confronting imposed governmental institutions and the approach dictated by maintaining Lakota identity and traditions. One example of this clash of beliefs is voting. The U.S. government assumes that positive self-governance must include voting as the key indicator of democratic principles. Many Lakotas, however, share the perspective that if you disagree with something, the way to express your dissent is to stay away from that event (Biolsi 1992:82). As a man from Manderson puts it: "No one believes in voting. It's only those people who have positions that go to the polls. Everybody else stays away. That was the traditional way of expressing your disapproval was to stay away." But when the point of disagreement is over the legitimacy of elections for officers, either within the tribal government or within county and state institutions, this Lakota form of political resistance has the opposite effect. Non-Indians walk away with the elections, attributing the low Lakota turnout to apathy, ignorance, and disinterest.

The imposed form of democracy also weakens traditional forms of deeper participatory, consensus-based government. Within the tribal government, the process of decision making is viewed as much different than in prereservation times. In the past, rather than express majority rule through voting, Lakotas debated issues at great length until they reached an agreement by consensus. If no agreement could be reached, the dissidents might separate into new *tiyóšpaye*. As one district representative noted, "In the old days, the council met for three or four days to make a decision. Now we have ten minutes." By truncating the decision-making process, outside interests in government and business can more easily obtain "tribal approval."

Although the Indian Reorganization Act of 1934 brought the promise of tribal self-government, the massive colonial-style bureaucratic administration of the BIA remains in place and continued to expand through the 1970s. The federal government enacted the Indian Self-Determination and Education Act of 1975, with the stated purpose of providing new avenues for asserting tribal interests and local needs. There was hope that the neocolonial relationship between the BIA and tribal governments would change when a preference was enforced for hiring Indians to fill BIA positions (Stubben 1994:113). Though the presence of more Indian employees at BIA desks diminishes the initial impression of a colonial administration, the power to determine the policies they enforce still lies beyond the reservations' boundaries. These employees are bound by the same federal regulations and procedures that their non-Indian predecessors had to follow. As a result, some Lakotas argue that changes in personnel only slightly increased the responsiveness of the BIA to local needs. Many Indian people work for the BIA but disagree with its overall control of reservation lives and economies. Yet scarce reservation jobs must be sacrificed to reduce the BIA presence on the reservation. Although the BIA has control over essential areas of reservation life, it is not elected by Lakotas in the way that similarly empowered local or state governments are. Rather, it is a bureaucratic manifestation of the combined interests of all constituencies across the United States, creating microlevel conditions for people they know nothing of or for whom they have no concern. Constituting only about 1 percent of the U.S. population, Indians have little or no elective control over this government apparatus, putting another twist in the application of the democratic process to Indian people.

The Indian Self-Determination and Education Act of 1975 made it possible for tribes to contract with the federal government to operate programs traditionally run by the BIA. Law enforcement, day school management, small business support, and the like can be transferred from the BIA to the tribal government through a process known as 638 contracting, derived from the provisions of Public Law 93–638 (Kalt and Cornell 1994: 147; Krepps 1995:181–83). Recent amendments to the act made it possible for tribes to contract to manage activities of other federal agencies within the Department of Interior, such as national park management. Conflicting "needs" of the local Lakota communities and the U.S. government are reflected in 638 contracting. The Lakotas' goal to enhance tribal self-determination often runs counter to the federal goal to reduce the financial and personnel needs of the BIA.

One of the major shortcomings of the contracting process is that the funds provided to the tribe under contract are significantly less than what the BIA itself would spend if it continued management of that department or program. None of the overhead costs that the BIA attributes to a program are included in the 638 contract amount, leaving tribes to perform more services with fewer resources. Furthermore, the administration of 638 contracts may bring minimal change to the structures of control over the tribe and its members. The BIA is still responsible for contract approval, oversight, and compliance review, leaving little leeway for real structural change in the tribe's approach to administration. Many of the philosophical issues of the approach or effects of a federally funded program do not change, regardless of who is managing that program (Bee and Gingerich 1977:86–87; Berglund 1979:4–5; Churchill 1994:40).

Many feel strongly that 638 contracting is designed for tribes to fail, thereby rejustifying the need for the BIA (McChesney 1992:109–11). The contracts themselves are massive, jargonistic, and replete with onerous financial and programmatic reporting requirements. Areas such as technical assistance for the management of programs are inadequate, with real BIA involvement coming only after problems have progressed beyond the point of no return. Finally, the expectations of tribal members are raised that substantial improvements will occur if a program is contracted, increasing the pressure for change and the disappointment if things stay the same.

Tribal governments often meet social and cultural needs that are not reflected in the efficiencies, order, and mainstream legal concepts that the BIA wants documented. Tribal governments ensure that Lakota cultural heritage is preserved and protected from exploitation and appropriation by outside entities. Reservations constitute social, cultural, and political homelands, where an otherwise excluded minority has self-determination, however limited, and the opportunity openly to express and experience what it means to be "Lakota" (Hoxie 1985; see Iverson 1975; Iverson 1981:164). Issues about jurisdiction, independence from state and federal oversight, and contracts with the federal government for Indian-run federal programs are the battlegrounds for larger concerns over political sovereignty and cultural autonomy. Lakotas living on the economic edge depend on the tribal government to watch out for the bigger picture of political and cultural preservation. As a Rosebud community activist notes, "It is a luxury on the reservation to not be absorbed in survival."

Tribal governments have a difficult role to play. Tribal leaders must aggressively assert social and political independence for the tribe while ensuring ongoing federal economic support (V. Deloria 1969:240–42; Hertzberg 1971:313; Hoxie 1985:70–72; McNickle 1973:113–14). When the tribe creates new programs responsive to local needs, their success is limited by insufficient federal financial support and the absence of other substantial sources of revenue. Some argue that tribal governments may not be effective in accomplishing their explicit purpose of providing self-governance to reservation communities but are good at meeting their personal needs or the needs of the broader economy (Churchill 1994: 48; see also Ferguson 1990). "The federal government and whoever else that try to help Indian people," a man from Manderson explains, "they always go through the tribal government, but that's the wrong approach, because the tribal government has been incredibly abusive toward the people. They spend all the money on themselves and nothing ever gets to the districts." Nowhere are the debates more heated than in the discussions of reservation economic development.

The Need for Economic Development

The issue of what is a "need" falls in the contested space of culture versus economic development. There are things that indigenous communities want, but they are not necessarily the needs assumed by economic development programs controlled by the dominant interests of the world economy (Escobar 1990; Hall 1989a:12–14; Jorgensen 1980:4; H. Moore 1992:136). Economic development has been attempted in many areas, but every project seems to end with similar results. The "needs" of these reservation communities become secondary to the "needs" of the dominant economy. Economic development programs sponsored by the federal government have consistently resulted in minimal improvements for the local economy but in direct benefits for outside interests of core capital, whether the programs are for human capital development, small business and microenterprise support, or agricultural and natural resource development.

Community Interpretations

The residents of Pine Ridge and Rosebud on the whole are extremely astute politically, having observed the impact of larger political and economic forces on their reservation economies for decades. In discussions about their perceptions of reservation economic development, Lakotas explicitly raise issues of colonialism, discrimination, and exploitation by forces beyond their community. A woman from St. Francis reflects this heightened awareness: "It is interesting that people are becoming more aware now of the effects of living and working with oppressive institutions on their own perspectives and attitudes. Six months ago you never heard about this internalized oppression, but now it comes up all the time. It's interesting, but I think it's a good thing." A woman from Rosebud feels it is important to "educate people on the institutional framework and its effects on the community. When you don't have power and control over law enforcement, social services, or the school system, it leads to the kind of violence, alcoholism, frustration, and exhaustion that we are experiencing here."

There is a basic contradiction between the expectations of the community and the commitment of the federal government in relation to economic development. Reservation residents look for programs to help change the causes of reservation poverty. The federal government, in contrast, provides services to the poor. A real change in reservation poverty would require fundamental alterations in the national economy and the commitment of a significant portion of the national income and resources for this purpose (Davidson and Levitan 1968:51; Donovan 1973:167, 179; Hamilton 1988:44; Piven and Cloward 1993:449–51). All indications are that this commitment is not forthcoming.

There is also a difference between national-level interpretations of what would be effective and local-level knowledge of what will work. Although there have been massive government studies of what is needed to improve the reservation community, virtually no support has been provided for the communities to develop their own conclusions. As a man from Kyle points out: "We don't have any shortage of ideas around here. It's the people in the community that know what's needed to solve our problems, not the people out there that end up controlling all the funds that come onto the rez. We need people who will support the people in their own ideas, who will listen rather than always talking about what's wrong with this place. People are doing their own things around here, they just don't get the big payoffs, they just get what they need to get by." A woman from Antelope adds: "You have a community that is basically tired of being studied and wants to have research that is addressing their needs from the inside." Those studies directed by national-level agencies tend to result in no long-term change, because there is no community ownership of the conclusions drawn.

The main question for the community, although it is often not included in the discussions between tribal officials and outside development concerns, centers on what form economic development should take. Some are ambivalent about the modernization model of industrial development, proposed most recently by President Clinton on his visit to Pine Ridge on July 6, 1999. A woman from Rosebud shares her hesitations:

> When I hear the term *economic development,* it makes me think of bringing in like big industry or smokestack buildings or whatever. Over the last two years, this big corporation has been working on Rosebud to try to make our land into like a waste landfill, so when I hear about economic development I think it's something we probably don't want to have, even though the economic conditions are poor, like probably the poorest in the country maybe after Pine Ridge. Our traditional values are not the same as the free enterprise system, and our culture isn't conducive to making a profit, that other things are more important and we don't want to turn our land into a landfill or necessarily have big industry take over our communities.

Others, like this elder man from Pine Ridge, express support for Lakota small business enterprises over locating large-scale multinational corporations on the reservation:

> I think if more people get interested in going the route of getting business started, what's going to make this place move toward self-sufficiency or whatever is going to have to be one person at a time. The tribe is always trying to put hundreds of people to work at one time, and then getting people's hopes up and the deal falls through, and you've got those hundreds of people feeling more and more like they'll never go to work at all. All that excitement and all that energy. But it's going to be small businesses, you know, putting one person themselves to work, or maybe themselves and one other person to work, that's what I think is going to work. If the tribe was to, by some miracle, actually land a big company, I think those days would be numbered for a big company like that.

A woman from Kyle challenges the materialist conception of well-being, asking: "What would make the people better off? Flush toilets? They are worse for the environment. People don't necessarily want what people on the outside think they should have."

From the perspective of reservation residents, free markets and competition are good for non-Indians, but as soon as Indians get involved in enterprise, state governments and non-Indian businesses demand federal government regulation of tribal economic undertakings. Wherever there has been tribal economic success, there has been federal regulation to ensure that the interests of the core are protected above tribal interests. When real decision-making authority remains out of the hands of the tribe, it skews economic benefits toward outside interests, not reservation economic development (Kalt and Cornell 1994:124–25).

Current legislative revisions and judicial interpretations of the Indian Gaming Act provide a vivid example of this lurking congressional power to appropriate tribal resources. The concern of non-Indians over competition and expanding tribal lands has multiplied with the development of Indian gaming. The October 17, 1988, Indian Gaming Regulatory Act was passed in response to the dramatic economic successes of several tribes in developing lucrative gaming and bingo operations on their reservations. With pressure from national gaming syndicates, Congress imposed massive oversight and approval requirements by the secretary of the interior onto tribes. Yet another federal entity, the National Indian Gaming Commission, was created to add another level of approval requirements for Indian gaming operation plans and revenue use. Most onerous of all, the act gave the states power over the continuation of certain Indian gaming enterprises by establishing a requirement of tribal-state compacts regarding permissible gaming activities (25 U.S. Code Sec. 2701–2721). A recent Ninth Circuit Appellate Court decision, *Rumsey Indian Rancheria v. Wilson,* determined that, although tribes are required to enter tribal-state compacts, states cannot be compelled to negotiate with tribes over specific forms of gaming activity (41 F.3d 421, 427 [9th Cir. 1994], *rehearing denied,* 64 F.3d 1250 [9th Cir. 1995], *cert. denied* by *Sycuan Band of Mission Indians v. Wilson* 117 S.Ct. 2508 [1997]). It is difficult to believe that this complex federal and state bureaucratic web will meet the stated purpose "to promote tribal economic development, tribal self-sufficiency, and strong tribal government" (25 U.S. Code 2701).

Both Pine Ridge and Rosebud have created tribal casinos, but the results to date have been modest at best. Such issues as location, management, regional competition, and the surrounding infrastructure of roads, restaurants, and hotels all play a role in the success of tribal gaming operations and will be critical to any long-term profits for Pine Ridge or Rosebud.

Federal Government Development Programs

The power to define political needs is intimately tied to the possession of significant financial resources. Although there is an extensive list of potential expenditures for tribal governments, the sources of tribal revenue are limited. The vast majority of funding for tribal governments has come directly from the U.S. government through federal grants. As a businessman from Rosebud asserts: "Money equates to sovereignty, so if the tribe wants to get to the point where it was really sovereign, it has to be financially sound." Many contend that actual control over tribal lands and resources and access to significant development capital are prerequisites to any genuine claim of tribal self-determination (Bee and Gingrich 1977:86–87; Berglund 1979:4–5; Churchill 1994:44).

Because of the uncertainty of tribal funding, many programs that the tribe starts are discontinued within a few years for lack of funding, as a woman from Antelope eloquently describes:

> There is a lot of work that needs to be done, and I think just looking at the time span there I think something should've at least come about by now, at least since the 1960s, something could've happened. But the tribe has got a lot of hoops it needs to jump through, the BIA being one of them. And then being stuck in the trap of that Bureau mentality. If you got hired in a job, you might be good for a year or for five years. If you get re-funded, you might have another three years to go, but then you have that program concept, so budgets are written in a way that you can't really be creative. It's all tied up and allocated in a way. So there is no room to do anything, just enough room to run programs.

Another tribal program officer notes: "When you work for the tribe, you have to show progress every couple of years or, even if there's no money, you got to show some progress or you'll lose your program. Even if you don't get anything, you have to use your ingenuity and try to serve more people. Anything you do, you have to be successful, you can't stagnate or they'll get rid of you."

Because of dependence on outside funding, tribes often do not control decisions about which programs should continue. Reservation residents become frustrated with the constant development of new government programs that people find beneficial, only to learn of their elimination two or three years later. "Programs are always developed in response to a crisis," a St. Francis man complains, "and then they fizzle out."

The War on Poverty in the 1960s generated the largest number of programs to help poor communities in general, and Indian communities specifically, since the New Deal in the 1930s. Pine Ridge was able to make initial gains in infrastructure and business development but was thwarted in the last stages of project implementation by funding delays and cuts (DeMallie 1978:298). Beginning with the presidency of Ronald Reagan and the Republican push to end big government, these programs were slowly dismantled one by one. Funding uncertainties and cutbacks mean that most programs are never able to mature beyond the startup phase (Bee 1981:138; Davidson and Levitan 1968:59). In discussing the strengths of the Office of Economic Opportunity (OEO) programs, one elder woman from Antelope notes: "I never was really involved too much in any of the development programs. I thought it was good when OEO came in, and I thought it should've stayed. What I don't like is a program comes in and is doing good, and then it runs out of funds and it seems like everything falls."

Interestingly, many of the government reservation economic development programs have been barely noticed by most of the reservation residents, calling into question the typical timelines that describe Lakota history in terms of federal programs. Though legislative debate and congressional action may fill the archives, without appropriations for implementation the effects of these policies on local-level economic conditions and development are limited at best.

Sporadic federal funding of ongoing reservation needs mirrors the economic cycles of the broader economy. In 1964, poverty spending, accompanied by a tax cut and economic expansion, seemed painless (Bee 1981:123; Donovan 1973:112). As the war in Vietnam intensified and economic prosperity lagged in the 1970s, OEO was funded with increasing resistance (Davidson and Levitan 1968:58–59, 82; Donovan 1973:63–64, 143, 153, 159; Hamilton 1988:35; Himmelman 1975:i, 5–7). In the face of recession followed by tepid economic growth, the Reagan administration called into question the entire mission of such agencies as the Department of Commerce, and the funding for special reservation support programs was erased under the banner of the end of big government and the virtues of self-sufficiency. With renewed confidence in the stock market and low unemployment, the Clinton administration now proposes "new" support for economic development in Pine Ridge.

Lakotas want programs that invest in their people through education and training. Yet many human capital development programs instituted on reservations do more for regional non-Indian employers than for the tribal trainees. The assumption behind job training has been that people are unemployed because they "need" job skills and experience, rather than because there are not enough local job opportunities. In fact, most reservation residents have some work experience. As noted in chapter 2, more than 90 percent of the Lakotas I spoke with had wage work experience, although 43 percent of them were currently unemployed. Only 14 percent of the unemployed Lakotas I spoke to had never held a wage labor job. Without local reservation job opportunities, trainees simply remain unemployed once their training period is complete or the training program is disbanded.

There is a long history of federal training programs in Pine Ridge and Rosebud. For example, the 1930s Indian Division of the Civilian Conservation Corps, discussed in chapter 4, was a job training and public works program extended to reservations under BIA supervision. The CCC-ID varied from the national program in several ways that limited the stated program goal of contributing to Lakota economic integration. Because poverty rates were so high on reservations, a job that went to a single man in the mainstream was divided in half and given to two possibly married men. Although the explanation for this practice was to spread the benefits of the CCC-ID through as much of the reservation community as possible, the married enrollees had a difficult time meeting their families' needs on the split program salary. Program administrators even justified having the families live in tents as part of their presumed inclination to live close to nature (Bromert 1978:345, 354–56; Parman 1971:43, 51).

Furthermore, the local CCC-ID projects to improve infrastructure or foster economic development ultimately ran to the greater benefit of the local non-Indian capital interests. Unlike other CCC teams, whose work projects were in part determined by the educational and training needs of the enrollees, the Indian Division had a rigorous list of projects whose completion had priority over any time taken for education or training. As a result, the CCC-ID had the greatest number of completed infrastructure improvements but provided almost no long-term benefits to the Indian enrollees. The projects, though within reservation boundaries, were intended to assist predominantly non-Indians leasing and raising cattle on reservation lands. Since the bulk of Lakota families had made the hard choice of leasing land for some cash rather than trying to raise cattle on inadequate acreage, the CCC projects in water development, irrigation, and soil erosion protection were not benefiting the impoverished local Lakota population (Bromert 1978:348, 350–51, 355; Parman 1971:46–49).

Current reservation job training programs raise similar questions of whether they are meeting the training needs of Lakota workers or the cheap labor needs of their employers. A woman from Rosebud describes the Joint Training Partnership Act, or JTPA: "The problem with that JTPA program is you hardly ever get hired after the training time is over. Even when they have an opening, they don't hire the JTPA trainees. After a thousand hours, they just let them go." A woman from Wanbli recalls: "When I was a soup kitchen aide, that was part of a jobs program. I worked four hours a day, but then after six months the government quit paying them the fifty dollars to hire me, they quit paying me and I wasn't about to do it for free." A woman from Kyle shares a similar experience: "I was in this Thousand Hour Program they called it. It would be JTPA now, but back then they called it NYC. I got training as a police dispatcher, but no job ever came of it. Once my hours were up, that was it." Now the work requirements of TANF have a similar ring. Welfare recipients are required to perform thirty hours of community service work to help them make the "transition" from welfare to work, but there are no real jobs on the reservations for these recipients to transition to (Pickering 2000). Lakotas are confronted with the choice of leaving the reservation to use their training, which defeats the purpose of developing the skills of the community, or becoming professional trainees, moving through one training program after another (Bee 1981:143, 146–47; Levitan and Johnston 1975: 12–13; Milkman 1972:304; Nolan 1967:1).

From the Lakota perspective, the reservations need more permanent full-time local jobs. The high incidence of seasonal and temporary wage labor jobs for Lakota workers acts as a subsidy to the surrounding economy. The severe underemployment of many Lakotas is a problem for the Lakota community, with more than half the employed residents of both Pine Ridge and Rosebud being employed for less than half the year. However, the easy availability of Lakota workers is a benefit for local employers, who are required to pay wages for only a few weeks a year. The costs of maintaining these temporary workers is borne by the Lakota community.

The Role of Microenterprise

As discussed in chapter 3, because of the unmet need for on-reservation wage labor jobs, many Lakota people supplement their incomes with microenterprise activities. Microenterprise in turn subsidizes wage workers, so they can afford to live on temporary, seasonal, and minimum wages from government and non-Indian concerns. Lakota microenterprise producers sell their items at depressed prices, allowing Lakota consumers to reserve their limited cash income for manufactured goods purchased from transnational corporate chains in border towns, such as Wal-Mart and Alco. As a result, most of the cash generated through wage work flows directly to consumer markets off the reservations. For example, plumbers and car mechanics charge people the cost of the parts purchased from off-reservation stores but then reduce or completely eliminate charges for their labor to make it affordable to the Lakota consumer.

Lakotas who produce traditional items create significant wealth for non-Indians dealing in the resale of Indian arts and crafts. Without capital for marketing beyond reservation boundaries, Lakota artisans must sell their products to local reservation shops that pay only one-quarter or less of the ultimate sales price but are always prepared to buy. Lakota producers of traditional items often feel exploited by these local operations, as a quilter from Oglala expresses: "They really take advantage of us, making their money off our work." A woman from Rosebud recalls one particular incident of exploitation: "This outstanding beader took a pair of moccasins [to a local tourist shop], they gave her the materials, but even so, they paid her $175, and then after our meeting we went back to that store and they had $785 on them, and they'll probably get that price from somebody, so I felt so bad. I wished that I could just sell them for her." Even the Catholic mission gift stores participate in the underpricing of traditional Lakota items, as a Manderson woman complains: "I took some stuff over to the Father when I needed some money pretty bad, and he only wanted to give me three dollars for earrings and four dollars for bracelets, so I told him to forget it, even if I did run out of gas before I made it home, that made me so mad. But they have just piles of this stuff that they've practically stolen off people. They don't pay nothing."

Slightly better prices are received from regional tourist shops in Rapid City or Denver. They have an ongoing demand for high-quality higher-priced beadwork, acting as middlemen for lucrative businesses in U.S. cities and European markets. Regional shops generally pay 50 percent of the ultimate sale price to the microenterprise producer. For example, a beadworker is paid $1,200 for a large beaded cradleboard, providing substantial income to the beader. The cradleboard is then sold through high-end beadwork and Indian art stores for $2,400. The best prices are received from national and international museums looking for high-quality beadwork reproductions of historic items. Those producing for the regional and national market try to demand at least ten dollars an hour for their labor but often settle for five. In contrast, taking average prices for supplies and hours per item, beadworkers make less than three dollars an hour for beadwork sold in the local reservation market. Lakota microenterprise producers must use their limited earnings for family needs, rather than their business "needs," such as more supplies or larger inventory. With this low compensation, some of the poorest reservation residents are providing substantial profits to off-reservation economic interests.

Agricultural Development

Land is one of the assets that Lakotas retained through the treaty process. Despite the rural character of the Pine Ridge and Rosebud Reservations, few Lakota households meet their economic needs through agriculture. The climate and terrain are best suited to ranching, but access to adequate land is a major barrier for Lakota ranchers. Though many Lakotas own some land, the original individual land allotments made on Pine Ridge and Rosebud between 1889 and 1910 have been fractionated through subsequent generations of heirs (Biolsi 1992:6). The small parcels of individual trust land tend to be insufficient to support a ranching operation. A man from Manderson hoping to start a ranching operation shares his experience of trying to remedy the heirship fractionation of his holdings: "I finally got all our fractionated land together to trade for a consolidated unit, and then one of my sisters opposed it. So even though I have land on the rez, I'm working on leasing a unit."

Most of those 5 percent of Lakota households from Pine Ridge and Rosebud involved in ranching on a full-time basis inherited their agricultural operations from their parents. A woman from Allen explains how her brother stayed in ranching: "When my dad passed away, then my mother lived up there [on their ranch] for maybe ten years. My brother moved in there and helped her until she passed away. My brother still lives up there." A Rosebud woman recalls a similar circumstance: "My parents ranched the whole time we were growing up, and then when they retired, my brother took over the ranching."

Most Lakota landowners must lease additional acres through the BIA for ranching or abandon agriculture and lease their lands out to other ranchers. Lakota ranchers encounter difficulties with the process of land leasing, as a woman from Rosebud explains: "The lease of land is hard, you have to pay so high for lease, and the land is broken down so bad. But they say that was masterminded from the Lincoln era. He knew that after so many generations it would be worthless to anyone, like to the heirs after six generations. So a lot of the land has whittled down to nothing. The land we live on we have to buy from the Farmers Home Administration, and then my husband inherited 160 acres from his dad, and then we lease the rest. It costs about six thousand dollars a year, from all different people. My husband moves the animals around. A lot of people will just abuse the land and overgraze it." The quality of land also affects the profitability of leasing land for ranching. A rancher from Kyle describes his land leasing: "I worked for about six years with my own units, but that unit bidding deal made it hard to get any land with decent water, so you end up losing all your money hauling your herd to water and back."

The BIA charges a minimal per acre amount to predominantly non-Indian ranchers leasing reservation trust lands. "I have some land that is leased out," an elder man from Kyle notes, "and I think I get five dollars a year for it. It's just like an ant trying to crawl on you, it's so small." Some Lakotas feel non-Indian ranchers have an advantage. "The BIA," a St. Francis rancher's wife explains, "they're a lot harder on Indian ranchers because they're there year after year so they're more visible than the others, but my husband, he always rotates. But some non-Indian ranchers will come in like just for the summer and just abuse the land, not hauling as much and stuff it full and eat it down, and then all you see is sunflowers the next year. And the BIA doesn't manage that land." A man from Wanbli concerned with wild plant conservation observes, "The more leasing out by BLM [U.S. Bureau of Land Management] for grazing, the less *thípsila* [wild turnips] there will be."

There is a BIA Indian preference program for land leasing on reservations, but Lakota ranchers are constrained by the way the preference is implemented. A man from Wounded Knee describes the program: "Indian preference means that an Indian can get a lease for land at the same price as the highest bidder for that unit. That can be tough on a guy trying to get a leg up in ranching." Lakotas need access to loans to compete successfully for leased land, but such funds are controlled by non-Indians, either the BIA or local private banks. As a result, it is difficult for Lakota families to become ranchers. As one Kyle man who wants to start a ranching operation explains: "There's a preference here for Indian people leasing land, so white people can't lease the land unless there are no Indian people who want to lease it for the same price. But for the Indian people they don't have the money it takes to get started, so even with the preference it ends up being mostly white ranchers." Furthermore, those who want to use their own lands sometimes have to wait for the current leaseholder to give up that land. As a man from Manderson told me: "My mom gave me 160 acres, but it's located on a unit that a white rancher is leasing and I can't displace him. I have to wait until he leaves or I can outbid him."

Tensions have always existed around the fact that the bulk of the treaty lands retained by the Lakotas have worked for the economic enrichment of non-Indians ranching on leased parcels of Indian land. "I would like to see the rez closed," a man from Manderson asserts, "so we could control who uses the land, and what cattle leave and stay. The way it is now, the ranchers take their cattle to Kansas, there they're slaughtered and sent to Chicago, and we buy it back from the Chicago wholesalers here. It's crazy. We don't have any control over our own economy." Lakota lands serve as a buffer for non-Indian ranchers when farm prices change. By having Indian lands available at low lease prices, ranchers can expand their operations in profitable periods and then contract in times of recession or low prices without having to make substantial investments in fixed land costs. At the same time, Lakota ranchers are marginal in good times and forced out of ranching production altogether in poor times (Carlson 1981:167; Hurt 1987:158–60, 183; Kelley 1979:37–41).

Natural Resource Development

The mineral resources within the current boundaries of the Pine Ridge and Rosebud Reservations are minimal. Nevertheless, the history behind the establishment of these boundaries reveals another set of competing needs between Lakotas and the world economy. The Black Hills have been a rich source of minerals such as gold, nickel, and uranium, as well as a popular natural attraction for tourists. Under the provisions of the Fort Laramie Treaty of 1868, the Lakotas retained ownership of the Black Hills. In the 1870s, gold was discovered there, and the region was overrun with white miners. Rather than enforce Lakota treaty rights, the U.S. government passed legislation in 1877 extinguishing Lakota title to the Black Hills.

In 1979, more than a century later, the U.S. Court of Claims recognized that the 1877 taking of Lakota land without compensation was a violation of the Fifth Amendment of the U.S. Constitution. The court awarded the Sioux Nation less than $50 million for this illegal taking and ruled that the United States was not liable for the gold extracted by trespassing miners because the government did not take the gold (*Sioux Nation of Indians v. U.S.*, 601 F.2d 1157 [Ct.Cl. 1979], *affirmed*, 448 U.S. 371,487 [1980]).

The Sioux Nation rejected the settlement and continues to hold out for congressional action to return the illegally taken land. From the perspective of the Lakotas, the Black Hills are central to their cultural and spiritual heritage, as well as an emblem of tribal sovereignty and treaty rights (Black Hills Alliance of South Dakota 1981:42; LaDuke and Churchill 1985:115). Furthermore, the land in question is still lucrative and productive for the world economy. The money settlement appears minuscule in light of the fact that in 1985 alone, $113 million in gold was extracted from the Black Hills (Bureau of Mines 1989:355). Senator Bill Bradley introduced a bill in Congress in 1985 to affirm the boundaries of the Great Sioux Reservation by conveying federally held lands in the Black Hills to the Sioux Nation (Fenelon 1998:223). The obvious significance of this proposed legislation to U.S. mining interests is confirmed by the discussion of this legislation in the U.S. Bureau of Mines's annual report on the mineral industry of South Dakota (Bureau of Mines 1989:357).

The millions of dollars of gold extracted from the Black Hills by private mining concerns since the 1860s are arguably Lakota resources exploited for no compensation to the Lakotas at all. This gold unquestionably contributed to capital accumulation by the dominant society and represents funds that would have significantly altered the economic conditions on the Lakota reservations if they had not been expropriated.

Uranium was also discovered in the Black Hills in the 1950s. Although the Lakotas received no financial benefit for uranium extraction from their rightful lands, they did receive the toxic effects of uranium mining. In 1962, two hundred tons of radioactive tailings washed into the Cheyenne River, polluting well water on the Pine Ridge Reservation. Disproportionate occurrences of miscarriage and other health effects were reported. The Lakotas had no control over these uranium operations taking place on lands illegally confiscated from them more than a century before (Black Hills Alliance of South Dakota 1981:46–49, 56–57; LaDuke and Churchill 1985:115–16, 119).

The economic balance between wealth and poverty would be easily shifted by a simple transfer in interest of the lands and resources that legally belong to the Lakotas. To date, the economic development needs of the Lakotas are not as important as the needs of dominant economic interests that continue to exploit these illegally held resources for mining, summer housing developments, and tourist enterprises.

Observers of the conditions on the Pine Ridge and Rosebud Reservations universally conclude that more economic development is necessary. After more than one hundred years of federal economic development programs, these reservation economies remain at the absolute bottom among U.S. counties. If Lakotas had the power to define their economic development needs, the history of these programs might be quite different. In practice, the economic development programs instituted have consistently enriched interests external to the reservation communities with little or no long-term effect on internal economic conditions.

The Need for Public Assistance

Because the benefits of Lakota economic activity are not enriching Lakota households, Lakota families are competing for small pools of federal public assistance dollars. Public assistance benefits have been and continue to be a tool used by the government to manipulate social change, though often not in the ways that are initially intended (Campbell 1993:64–66).

From the time the reservations were formed in the 1880s, BIA agents used rations and other supports to promote Lakota compliance with government policies and to encourage Lakota families to become small-scale farmers, in the image of white settlers (Biolsi 1992:18). Lakota horse herds were confiscated by the U.S. government and destroyed as an impediment to agriculture and "civilization" (Mooney 1896:837). Agents suggested that ration supports be terminated to threaten reservation residents with actual starvation, rather than simple malnutrition, to force the Lakotas to abandon their communal approach to production and consumption (Mekeel 1936:13).

After World War II, public assistance was virtually ended, to encourage Lakota workers to enter the growing agricultural and industrial economy. Many Lakotas worked in the fields as young people because there was little or no welfare in the 1950s and 1960s. An elder man from Kyle recalls: "There wasn't much relief in my time like there is now. When I was first married, I tried to get grant, but I never got anything, and then when we did get it, it wasn't enough, so I went to Nebraska and all over looking for work."

The new welfare reform legislation continues the policy of manipulating economic behavior with the threat of starvation. TANF requires that welfare recipients find wage work or lose their benefits. However, the Lakotas are living in labor markets with no wage jobs. As a result, the only remaining alternatives are further reducing already minimal household needs or leaving the reservation for wage work (Pickering 2000).

The politics of food in defining Lakota need has been important since the reservations were formed. The early economy of the Dakota Territory was so shaky from extended drought that U.S. government contracts to supply the Lakota and other Indian reservations with annuities and rations were a major source of income for Dakota settlers (Lamar 1956: 108, 284; Limerick 1987:83–84). When the secretary of the interior tried to investigate corruption in these contracts, the entire territorial government and settlers protested, stonewalling the inquiry (Lamar 1956:108–8). In the 1930s and 1940s, the government purchased surplus commodities from non-Indian growers across the United States to support farm prices and then distributed them to Indian families as food aid (Macgregor 1946.48, Mekeel 1936:10; Wissler 1938:60–61).

Currently, food need is defined by the broader economy as surplus produce farmers need to sell or grocery items wholesalers have been unable to sell. The national commodities program sponsored by the U.S. Department of Agriculture has been promoted for its role in preventing hunger in poor U.S. communities, but it has also supplied income to farmers and food producers for their surplus produce. A nonprofit food bank provides foods donated by corporations for tax write-offs to help needy households. The foods provided have little to do with locally defined food needs. "Food Bank you're eligible every other month," a woman from Oglala receiving food subsidies explains. "I usually don't use all that fancy food — they have frozen food, and they have pizza pockets that one time. But they have Tide soap and hand soap, that comes in handy."

Lakotas commonly believe that these public assistance programs are a form of long-term reciprocity managed by the government. First, the long history of treaty rights and U.S. government trust responsibility toward the Lakota tribes established a set of services owed the people over time in exchange for the large-scale land transfers the Lakotas made to the U.S. government (Biolsi 1992:17, 32). Specific provisions of such treaties as the Fort Laramie Treaty of 1868 made a commitment to providing health, education, and food supports to Lakota people. Though today's government agencies do not consider federal assistance programs to be legislatively related to these treaties, many Lakota people draw a relationship between the two. Current public assistance benefits are viewed as merely the latest form of treaty annuities and rations due and owing to the descendants of the Lakota treaty negotiators. Furthermore, the amounts provided in welfare benefits are minimal in comparison with the government subsidies provided to non-Indian ranching, mining, and industrial interests that have benefited from extracting surplus Lakota resources and labor at varying times in the economic history of the reservations.

Some Lakotas hold a second view of welfare: that it is a benefit paid for by relatives who were able to find full-time employment. A person should be entitled to receive various forms of public assistance if she has a close relative who had a wage work job and paid into the income tax, Social Security, and unemployment systems. The welfare recipient is simply receiving benefits that have been more than covered by the wage work of her relatives.

Despite the attitude of entitlement, there is still considerable disappointment with the incentives that public assistance creates for reservation residents. Those who have been successful in the mainstream economy are the most supportive of the work requirements of welfare reform. "Giving them welfare I think is just hurting their initiative," according to a self-made Lakota businessman from Pine Ridge, "not helping them to realize their potential. Until you're willing to invest in people, things are just going to stay the way they are. I think the education should start right in school. They should give the kids a week's worth of tokens for lunch, and if they want to spend it on candy or buy their friends lunch or whatever they can, but if they run out, they don't eat. That's how people learn, not by having everything handed to them regardless. That's really held our people back, and kept them from learning how to work in the system."

Many people express frustration with the level of pure bureaucracy standing between Lakotas and the government programs allegedly designed to assist them. One woman summarizes it quite directly: "Getting the run-around is part of the system. These institutions are not intended to meet people's needs, they are part of a system of applied racism. The institutional framework affects you when you don't have power and control over it. You feel frustrated at the end of the week when you have to go out to four or five institutions and confront your own people gatekeeping. Even if the gatekeepers aren't personally racist, they are implementing racist policies every time they participate in perpetuating the run-around."

Defining and satisfying needs is a profoundly political process. A century of federal Indian policy, ostensibly designed to meet the needs of the Lakotas, has usually satisfied instead the needs of core interests outside these reservation communities. Improvements in Lakotas' well-being will come only when the political will of the core is changed to allow economic control and growth for these peripheral reservation communities.

Conclusion

Lakota culture influences how residents of the Pine Ridge and Rosebud Reservations experience incorporation in the world economy in their day-to-day lives. Lakota households confront issues of production and consumption within the world economy with distinctly Lakota ideals, values, and priorities. Even in the most market-based forms of production, Lakota culture plays a hand in shaping the reactions to, participation in, and resistance to the world economy. In wage work settings, Lakota values provide a basis for questioning the benefits of low-paying, boring, dangerous, or distant job opportunities. The importance of family obligations and community commitments is raised and defended in the face of workplaces driven by the economic and political priorities of the world economy. When the imposed conditions of wage work become too onerous, Lakota culture provides a social safety net that offers support between jobs and connections for new jobs. Local concerns of Lakota culture struggle against structural and managerial requirements imposed by the world economy, as illustrated in the experiences of Lakota nonprofit organizations. Lakota business people meet the challenge of conforming to management principles and practices of the world economy while complying with local cultural conventions of behaving like a good relative, such as Indian pricing, employing family members, and respecting egalitarian principles for the community.

Although the world economy limits access to market-based economic activity, Lakota culture plays a role in providing social networks for alternative forms of production. Households engage in time-consuming but inexpensive forms of production for direct consumption, exchanging labor, goods, and services within an extended network of social relationships. Microenterprise producers fill the gaps left by inadequate wage work opportunities in the periphery while reinforcing cultural values of self-sufficiency, industry, and sharing. Through displays of generosity and sacrifice for the greater good, ceremonial events and religious practices also provide economic support to community members. These alternative forms of production are not independent of the forces of the world economy but in effect subsidize the market economy, as household production makes survival on low wages possible. Household production takes time, space, and energy from household members with little or no compensation, and household producers increasingly respond to the demands of outside middlemen to meet the production schedules and supply the items attractive to non-Indian markets.

The Lakotas' position within the world economy prevents the type of specialization that the mainstream economy requires. As in the pre-reservation economy, each person must perform multiple and diverse roles simultaneously and over time, roles that coalesce into one living. Because each person is involved in management, maintenance, counseling, clothing, and shelter, his or her efforts are never rewarded by the larger economic system, which values specialization and expertise. Wage laborers supplement their incomes with small business, microenterprise, and hunting and gathering. Those who are unemployed place greater emphasis on microenterprise, hunting and gathering, and other temporary and irregular self-employment. Those remaining in agriculture find limited access to capital and to adequate land and are pushed toward wage labor income supplementation. The market relations of wage labor, limited agricultural sales, and small business transactions are complemented with reciprocal relations of family-based production, lending from family and friends, variable pricing in response to individual means and needs, and nonmonetary exchanges of services and goods.

Even the realm of cash consumption exhibits the tensions between the inducements of the world economy and the protections of local culture. Participation in the cash economy has increased, not only as a result of growing Lakota demand for consumer goods but also as a result of federal policies and programs that require greater uses of cash. At the same time, social support networks and cultural norms against materialism minimize the emotional connections between cash consumption and Lakota concepts of well-being.

In other ways, the Lakotas' situation is no different from that of hundreds of other indigenous societies in rural, peripheral areas within the world economy (Hall 1996; Hall 1989b; Snipp 1986). Many of the opportunities and constraints that confront these Lakota communities are not unique to the American Indian experience but in fact mirror trends in the broader economic experiences of other minority groups in the United States. For example, African-American households living in U.S. urban centers but systematically excluded from secure and well-paying forms of wage labor use kin-based social networks and alter-

native forms of economic activity similar to those of Lakota communities as survival strategies (Stack 1974; Wilson 1996, 1987). Cultural
communities in the economic periphery of Latin America and Africa perform kin-based household subsistence activities to subsidize the support
of wage workers paid less than a living wage by multinational corporations (Bradby 1980; Frank 1966; Gimenez 1988; Meillassoux 1981; Obregon 1980; Rodney 1972). In these contexts, poverty is the result of participating in the "opportunities" offered by the world economy, not of
being isolated from the world economy. The tremendous uncertainty of
the economic support offered by the world economy makes kin-based
social networks and cultural forms of economic redistribution essential
to survival. If we acknowledge incorporation as a cultural process, we
can account for the way culture produces adaptive strategies that make
survival feasible within the constraints of the world system.

Economic incorporation of local cultures into the world system is an
ongoing dynamic that is subject to reversal and resistance (Hall 1989a:
17–23; 1989b:224–25). After periods of extensive and intensive colonial
control, indigenous peoples have emerged ready to bring their traditions back out of the closet of administrative oppression (Dunaway 1996;
Fischer and Brown 1996). Given the spaces created by local culture to
avoid or diminish the impact of world-system incorporation, core capital faces the challenge of maintaining incorporation even in periods of
limited interest in the labor or resources of a particular peripheral area.

The world economy has mechanisms for maintaining the incorporation of the periphery on a day-to-day basis. These mechanisms lack the
drama of conquest or the intensity of active resource exploitation but
nevertheless continue the flow of benefits from small-scale transactions to
the core beneficiaries of the world economy. The first is the manipulation
of social identities. Social identities of gender, ethnicity, tribal membership, and race all play a role in the access Lakotas have to market opportunities and the returns they receive from market participation. Legitimate
debates about the proper balance between economic and cultural via-
bility embody contemporary configurations of Lakota values and beliefs,
informed by internal identities of age, gender, ethnicity, and class.

The negative social identity of being Indian constrains external economic opportunities for Lakota communities and denies them the surplus that their labor and resources produce. There is no obvious de-
marcation between the impact of ethnicity or culture and the impact of
occupying a marginal niche within the world economy, however. Local
non-Indian ranchers or tourist hotel owners who exploit Indian land or
laborers in turn are exploited by larger commodity markets and hotel

franchise corporations, contributing ultimately to the accumulation of international capital that fuels further expansion of the world economy. Better understanding of the cultural beliefs and values of non-Indian households surrounding the Lakotas would help clarify those aspects of poverty that are dictated by the peripheral position of these small, isolated rural communities, independent of culturally based attitudes and practices.

The second mechanism for maintaining control over the periphery is the political and economic power of the core to define needs in the periphery. Federal policies of Indian self-governance, economic development, and public assistance have continuously and repeatedly resulted in limited benefits for Lakota community members and significant benefits for core capital outside the reservation boundaries. The core's shifting interests in Lakota labor and resources have a direct effect on the economic opportunities of Lakota communities. Lakota wage labor migration for the Civilian Conservation Corps, agricultural interests, and urban relocation had its roots in each case in labor demands by core capital. When the national demand for unskilled labor declines, the extent of Lakota wage labor participation also declines and microenterprise and other forms of self-employment begin to flourish.

The need of the world economy for natural resources outweighed the needs of the Lakotas for cultural preservation of sacred sites and self-determination over the territory delineated to them through treaty negotiations. Core demands for access to land precipitated the land allotment policies that substantially reduced the landmass of both reservations. BIA management of land and low lease rates serve as a buffer for shifts in the agricultural economy of neighboring non-Indian farmers and ranchers, as do the remaining short-term seasonal farmhands.

The Lakotas' need for jobs, household income, and access to land, capital, and natural resources has been outweighed by the need of the interests of core capital for inexpensive and convenient labor, capital accumulation, agricultural subsidization, and low-cost mining operations. Unless the political power to define need shifts toward these Lakota communities, economic development that will benefit reservation residents will remain out of reach.

Although culture is not independent of the world economy, it plays a role in shaping the path of that world economy. Cultural forms of resistance may not prevent the accumulation of surplus by core interests. At the same time, incorporation into the world economy does not dictate the end of local cultures. It is the dynamic tension between local culture and the world economy that ultimately produces both the contemporary configurations of local cultures and the trajectory of the current world economy.

Appendix 1
Summary of Formal
Interview Participants

Characteristic	Pine Ridge	Rosebud	Total
Gender			
Men	22	13	35
Women	38	27	65
Age			
21 years or less	0	2	2
22–34	12	6	18
35–49	30	18	48
50–64	14	10	24
65 and older	4	4	8
Work activity			
Full-time wage worker	15	12	27
Part-time/seasonal/temporary wage	18	12	30
Not a wage worker	27	16	43
Small business owner	19	16	35
Microentrepreneur	35	23	58
Rancher	6	5	11
Involved in subsistence activities	20	11	31
Cash benefit recipient	29	19	48
Wage worker in past	58	32	90
Off-reservation wage worker in past	39	28	67
Education			
8th grade or less	8	3	11
9th–11th grade	8	4	12
High school graduate	16	9	25
Some college work	20	14	34
Bachelor's degree	8	5	13
More than bachelor's degree	0	5	5

Appendix 2
Number of People Interviewed, by Community

Community	No. of people interviewed
Pine Ridge Reservation	
Pine Ridge Village	14
Kyle	16
Wanbli/Potato Creek	13
Oglala	8
Wounded Knee/Manderson	6
Porcupine	3
Total	60

Community	No. of people interviewed
Rosebud Reservation	
Rosebud Village	16
Mission/Antelope	16
St. Francis	5
Parmelee	3
Total	40

Bibliography

Adams, David. 1995. *Education for Extinction: American Indians and the Boarding School Experience, 1875–1928*. Lawrence: University Press of Kansas.

Albers, Patricia C. 1985. Autonomy and Dependency in the Lives of Dakota Women: A Study in Historical Change. *Review of Radical Political Economics* 17(3): 109–34.

———. 1983. Sioux Women in Transition: A Study in Their Changing Status in Domestic and Capitalist Sectors of Production. In *The Hidden Half*, edited by Patricia Albers and Beatrice Medicine, 175–236. Lanham MD: University Press of America.

———. 1982. Sioux Kinship in a Colonial Setting. *Dialectical Anthropology* 6: 253–69.

Anders, Gary C. 1980. Theories of Underdevelopment and the American Indian. *Journal of Economic Issues* 14(3): 681–701.

Appadurai, Arjun. 1990. Disjuncture and Difference in the Global Cultural Economy. *Theory, Culture, and Society* 7:295–310.

Bailey, Ronald, and Guillermo Flores. 1973. Internal Colonialism and Racial Minorities in the U.S. In *Structures of Dependency*, edited by Frank Bonilla and Robert Girling, 149–60. Palo Alto CA: Stanford University.

Bamforth, Douglas B. 1988. *Ecology and Human Organization on the Great Plains*. New York: Plenum Press.

Beauvais, Fred. 1998. American Indians and Alcohol. *Alcohol Health and Research World* 22(4): 253–59.

Bee, Robert L. 1981. *Crosscurrents along the Colorado: The Impact of Government Policy on the Quechan Indians*. Tucson: University of Arizona Press.

Bee, Robert, and Ronald Gingerich. 1977. Colonialism, Classes, and Ethnic Identity: Native Americans and the National Political Economy. *Studies in Comparative International Development* 12: 70–93.

Berglund, Staffan. 1979. *The New Indianism: A Threat against Imperialism and Underdevelopment*. Research Reports, Department of Sociology, no. 54. Umea, Sweden: University of Umea.

Biolsi, Thomas. 1992. *Organizing the Lakota*. Tucson: University of Arizona Press.

Black Hills Alliance of South Dakota. 1981. *Keystone to Survival: The Multinational Corporations and the Struggle for Control of Land*. Rapid City SD: Black Hills Alliance.

Blacks Hills State College. 1975. *American Indian Political Systems.* Spearfish SD: Black Hills State College, Center of Indian Studies.

Blakeslee, Donald J. 1981. Toward a Cultural Understanding of Human Micro-evolution on the Great Plains. *Plains Anthropologist* 26(92): 93–106.

———. 1977. The Calumet Ceremony and the Origin of Fur Trade Rituals. *Western Canadian Journal of Anthropology* 7(2): 78–89.

Boris, Eileen, and Elisabeth Prugl, eds. 1996. *Homeworkers in Global Perspective.* New York: Routledge.

Bradby, Barbara. 1980. The Destruction of Natural Economy. In *The Articulation of Modes of Production,* edited by Harold Wolpe, 93–127. London: Routledge & Kegan Paul.

Bromert, Roger. 1978. The Sioux and the Indian-CCC. *South Dakota History* 8(4): 340–56.

Browne, Katherine E. 1997. The Economic Immobility of Women in Martinique. *Research in Economic Anthropology* 18:183–216.

Bucko, Raymond. 1998. *The Lakota Ritual of the Sweat Lodge.* Lincoln: University of Nebraska Press.

Bureau of Indian Affairs (BIA). Statistics, 1988–1991. Household Income and Un-employment Statistics. Rosebud and Pine Ridge Agencies, South Dakota: U.S. Government.

Bureau of Mines, U.S. Department of Interior. 1989. *Minerals Yearbook 1987,* vol. 2. Washington DC: U.S. Government Printing Office.

Burgess, Thomas. 1991. Wage Labor Lost: Silent History of the Lakota. Paper presented at the American Anthropological Association 90th Annual Meeting, November 20–24, Washington DC.

Cahn, Edgar S., ed. 1970. *Our Brother's Keeper: The Indian in White America.* New York: New Community Press.

Campbell, Gregory. 1993. Health Patterns and Economic Underdevelopment on the Northern Cheyenne Reservations, 1910–1920. In *The Political Economy of North American Indians,* edited by John Moore, 60–86. Norman: University of Oklahoma Press.

Canby, William C., Jr. 1983. *American Indian Law.* St. Paul: West Publishing Co.

Carlson, Leonard. 1981. *Indians, Bureaucrats, and the Land: The Dawes Act and the Decline of Indian Farming.* Westport CT: Greenwood Press.

Cash, Joseph H., and Herbert T. Hoover, eds. 1971. *To Be an Indian: An Oral History.* New York: Holt, Rinehart & Winston.

Castile, George, and Robert Bee. 1992. Introduction. In *State and Reservation: New Perspectives on Federal Indian Policy,* edited by George Castile and Robert Bee, 1–9. Tucson: University of Arizona Press.

Child, Brenda. 1998. *Boarding School Seasons: American Indian Families, 1900–1940.* Lincoln: University of Nebraska Press.

Churchill, Ward. 1994. American Indian Self-Governance: Fact, Fantasy, and Prospects for the Future. In *American Indian Policy: Self-Governance and Eco-*

nomic Development, edited by Lyman Legters and Fremont Lyden, 37–53. Westport CT: Greenwood Press.

Colorado Department of Labor. 1991. *Affirmative Action* (booklet). Denver: State of Colorado.

Cornell, Stephen. 1988. *The Return of the Native: American Indian Political Resurgence*. New York: Oxford University Press.

Davidson, Roger H., and Sar Levitan. 1968. *Antipoverty Housekeeping: The Administration of the Economic Opportunity Act*. Ann Arbor: Institute of Labor and Industrial Relations.

Deloria, Ella. 1944. *Speaking of Indians*. New York: Friendship Press.

Deloria, Vine, Jr. 1969. *Custer Died for Your Sins*. London: Collier-Macmillan.

Deloria, Vine, Jr., and Clifford Lytle. 1984. *The Nations Within*. New York: Pantheon.

DeMallie, Raymond. 1984. *The Sixth Grandfather: Black Elk's Teachings Given to John G. Neihardt*. Lincoln: University of Nebraska Press.

———. 1979. Change in American Indian Kinship Systems: The Dakota. In *Currents in Anthropology: Essays in Honor of Sol Tax*, edited by Robert Hinshaw, 221–41. The Hague: Mouton.

———. 1978. Pine Ridge Economy: Cultural and Historical Perspectives. In *American Indian Economic Development*, edited by Sam Stanley, 237–312. Chicago: Aldine.

DeMallie, Raymond, and Douglas Parks, eds. 1987. *Sioux Indian Religion*. Norman: University of Oklahoma Press.

Denig, Edwin Thompson. 1961. *Five Indian Tribes of the Upper Missouri*, edited by John C. Ewers. Norman: University of Oklahoma Press.

Denver Labor Statistics. 1991. *American Indian Workforce Participation*. Denver: State of Colorado.

Dewing, Rolland. 1985. *Wounded Knee: The Meaning and Significance of the Second Incident*. New York: Irvington.

Diamant, Adam. 1988. *Economic Development: The Rosebud Sioux Indian Tribe*. Harvard Project on American Indian Economic Development. Cambridge MA: Harvard University.

Donovan, John C. 1973. *The Politics of Poverty*. Indianapolis: Bobbs-Merrill.

Dorsey, James Owen. 1897. Siouan Sociology. *15th Annual Report of the Bureau of Ethnology, 1893–94*. Washington DC: U.S. Government Printing Office.

Dunaway, Wilma. 1996. Incorporation as an Interactive Process: Cherokee Resistance to Expansion of the Capitalist World-System, 1560–1762. *Sociological Inquiry* 66(4): 455–70.

Ellis, Clyde. 1996. *To Change Them Forever: Indian Education at the Rainy Mountain Boarding School, 1893–1920*. Norman: University of Oklahoma Press.

Escobar, Arturo. 1990. Anthropology and the Development Encounter: The Making and Marketing of Development Anthropology. *American Ethnologist* 18(4): 658–82.

Ewers, John C. 1968. *Indian Life on the Upper Missouri.* Norman: University of Oklahoma Press.

Fay, George E. 1967. *Charters, Constitutions, and By-Laws of the Indian Tribes of North America. Part I: The Sioux Tribes of South Dakota.* Greeley: Colorado State College.

Federal Archives Research Center (FARC). Record Group 75. U.S. Pine Ridge Agency Records. Kansas City MO.

———. Record Group 75. U.S. Rosebud Agency Records. Kansas City MO.

Fenelon, James. 1998. *Culturicide, Resistance, and Survival of the Lakota ("Sioux Nation").* New York: Garland.

Feraca, Stephen. 1998. *Lakota Religion in the Twentieth Century.* Lincoln: University of Nebraska Press.

Ferguson, James. 1990. *The Anti-Politics Machine.* New York: Cambridge University Press.

Fischer, Edward, and R. McKenna Brown. 1996. *Maya Cultural Activism in Guatemala.* Austin: Texas University Press.

Frank, Andre Gunder. 1966. The Development of Underdevelopment. *Monthly Review* 18:17–31.

Fraser, Nancy. 1989. *Unruly Practices: Power, Discourse, and Gender in Contemporary Social Theory.* Minneapolis: University of Minnesota Press.

Frazier, Ian. 1999. On the Rez. *Atlantic Monthly* 284 (December): 53–84.

Gimenez, Martha E. 1988. Minorities and the World-System: Theoretical and Political Implications of the Internationalization of Minorities. In *Racism, Sexism, and the World-System,* edited by Joan Smith, Jane Collins, Terence L. Hopkins, and Akbar Muhammad, 39–56. New York: Greenwood Press.

Goldfrank, Esther S. 1943. Historic Change and Social Character: A Study of the Teton Dakota. *American Anthropologist* 45(1): 67–83.

Graves, Theodore. 1971. Drinking and Drunkenness among Urban Indians. In *The American Indian in Urban Society,* edited by Jack O. Waddell and O. Michael Watson, 274–311. Boston: Little, Brown.

Grobsmith, Elizabeth. 1981. *Lakota of the Rosebud: A Contemporary Ethnography.* New York: Holt, Rinehart & Winston.

Hall, Thomas D. 1996. The World-System Perspective: A Small Sample from a Large Universe. *Sociological Inquiry* 66(4): 440–54.

———. 1989a. *Social Change in the Southwest, 1350–1880.* Lawrence: University Press of Kansas.

———. 1989b. Historical Sociology and Native Americans: Methodological Problems. *American Indian Quarterly* 13(3): 223–38.

Hamilton, David. 1988. Poverty Is Still with Us — and Worse. In *Quiet Riots: Race and Poverty in the United States,* edited by Fred Harris and Roger W. Wilkins, 29–45. New York: Pantheon.

Hanson, James A. 1975. *Metal Weapons, Tools, and Ornaments of the Teton Dakota Indians.* Lincoln: University of Nebraska Press.

Hargreaves, Margaret Barnwell, and Hedy Nai-Lin Chang. 1989. *Evaluating the*

Impact of Federal Welfare Reform in Indian Country: A Case Study of the Rosebud Sioux Reservation. Harvard Project on American Indian Economic Development. Cambridge MA: Harvard University.

Hassrick, Royal. 1964. *The Sioux.* Norman: University of Oklahoma Press.

Henning, Elizabeth R. P. 1982. Western Dakota Winter Counts: An Analysis of the Effects of Westward Migration and Culture Change. *Plains Anthropologist* 27(97): 57–65.

Hertzberg, Hazel W. 1971. *The Search for an American Indian Identity: Modern Pan-Indian Movements.* Syracuse: University of Syracuse Press.

Hickson, Harold. 1974. *Sioux Indians I: Mdewakanton Band of Sioux Indians.* New York: Garland.

Himmelman, Harold. 1975. *The Fall and Rise of the Office of Economic Opportunity.* Washington DC: Lawyers' Committee for Civil Rights under Law.

Hindess, Barry, and Paul Q. Hirst. 1975. *Pre-Capitalist Modes of Production.* London: Routledge & Kegan Paul.

Holder, Preston. 1970. *The Hoe and the Horse on the Plains.* Lincoln: University of Nebraska Press.

Howard, James H. 1960. The Cultural Position of the Dakota: A Reassessment. In *Essays in the Science of Culture: In Honor of Leslie A. White,* edited by Gertrude Dole and Robert Carneiro, 249–68. New York: Thomas Y. Crowell.

Hoxie, Frederick E. 1985. From Prison to Homeland: The Cheyenne River Reservation before World War I. In *Plains Indians of the Twentieth Century,* edited by Peter Iverson, 55–75. Norman: University of Oklahoma Press.

Hurt, R. Douglas. 1987. *Indian Agriculture in America: Prehistory to Present.* Lawrence: University of Kansas Press.

Hyde, George E. 1961. *Spotted Tail's Folk: A History of the Brule Sioux.* Norman: University of Oklahoma Press.

———. 1956. *Sioux Chronicle.* Norman: University of Oklahoma Press.

———. 1937. *Red Cloud's Folk: A History of the Oglala Sioux Indians.* Norman: University of Oklahoma Press.

Iverson, Peter. 1994. *When Indians Became Cowboys.* Norman: University of Oklahoma Press.

———. 1981. *The Navajo Nation.* Westport CT: Greenwood Press.

———. 1975. The Rise of Navajo Nationalism. In *Identity and Awareness in the Minority Experience,* edited by George Carter and Bruce Mouser, 85–107. Lacrosse: Institute for Minority Studies, University of Wisconsin.

Johnston, Sister Mary Antonio. 1948. *Federal Relations with the Great Sioux Indians of South Dakota, 1887–1933.* Washington DC: Catholic University of America Press.

Jorgensen, Joseph. 1980. A Century of Political Economic Effects on American Indian Society, 1880–1980. *Journal of Ethnic Studies* 6(3): 1–82.

———. 1971. Indians and the Metropolis. In *The American Indian in Urban Society,* edited by Jack O. Waddell and O. Michael Watson, 66–113. Boston: Little, Brown.

Junglas, Laura, and Peter Barringer. 1989. *Rosebud Reservation Enterprise Center: Feasibility Analysis and Development Plan.* Boston: Neighborhood Reinvestment Corporation.

Kalt, Joseph, and Stephen Cornell. 1994. The Redefinition of Property Rights in American Indian Reservations: A Comparative Analysis of North American Economic Development. In *American Indian Policy: Self-Governance and Economic Development,* edited by Lyman Legters and Fremont Lyden, 121–50. Westport CT: Greenwood Press.

Kehoe, Alice Beck. 1989. *The Ghost Dance: Ethnohistory and Revitalization.* Chicago: Holt, Rinehart & Winston.

Kehoe, Thomas F. 1983. A Retrospective and Commentary. In *From Microcosm to Macrocosm: Advances in Tipi Ring Investigation and Interpretation,* edited by Leslie B. Davis. *Plains Anthropologist* 28 (102, pt. 2), Memoir 19:327–42.

Kelley, Klara B. 1979. Federal Indian Land Policy and Economic Development in the United States. In *Economic Development in American Indian Reservations,* edited by Roxanne Dunbar. Native American Studies, University of New Mexico. Albuquerque: University of New Mexico.

Kelly, Fanny Wiggins. 1962. *My Captivity among the Sioux Indians.* New York: Corinth Books.

Kenner, Charles. 1969. *A History of New Mexican–Plains Indian Relations.* Norman: University of Oklahoma Press.

Klein, Alan. 1983. The Political-Economy of Gender: A Nineteenth-Century Plains Indian Case Study. In *The Hidden Half: Studies of Plains Indian Women,* edited by Patricia Albers and Beatrice Medicine, 143–73. Lanham MD: University Press of America.

Krepps, Matthew. 1995. Can Tribes Manage Their Own Resources? The 638 Program and American Indian Forestry. In *What Can Tribes Do? Strategies and Institutions in American Indian Economic Development,* edited by Stephen Cornell and Joseph Kalt, 179–203. Los Angeles: American Indian Studies Center, University of California.

Kroeber, Alfred L. 1939. *Cultural and Natural Areas of Native North America.* Berkeley: University of California Press.

LaDuke, Winona, and Ward Churchill. 1985. Native America: The Political Economy of Radioactive Colonialism. *Journal of Ethnic Studies* 13(3): 107–32.

Lamar, Howard R. 1956. *Dakota Territory, 1861–1889: A Study of Frontier Politics.* New Haven: Yale University Press.

Levitan, Sar, and William B. Johnston. 1975. *Indian Giving: Federal Programs for Native Americans.* Baltimore: Johns Hopkins University Press.

Lewis, Thomas H. 1990. *The Medicine Men: Oglala Sioux Ceremony and Healing.* Lincoln: University of Nebraska Press.

Limerick, Patricia. 1987. *The Legacy of Conquest: The Unbroken Past of the American West.* New York: W. W. Norton.

Littlefield, Alice. 1996. Indian Education and the World of Work in Michigan, 1893–1933. In *Native Americans and Wage Labor: Ethnohistorical Perspectives,* edited by Alice Littlefield and Martha Knack, 100–121. Norman: University of Oklahoma Press.

————. 1993. Learning to Labor: Native American Education in the United States, 1880–1930. In *The Political Economy of North American Indians,* edited by John Moore, 43–59. Norman: University of Oklahoma Press.

Macgregor, Gordon. 1946. *Warriors without Weapons.* Chicago: University of Chicago Press.

Mallery, Garrick. 1893. Picture-Writing of the American Indians. *10th Annual Report of the Bureau of Ethnology, 1888–89.* Washington DC: U.S. Government Printing Office.

Marquette University Library Archives. 1914. Bureau of Catholic Mission Records. Milwaukee WI.

Matthiessen, Peter. 1980. *In the Spirit of Crazy Horse.* New York: Viking Press.

May, Philip. 1996. Overview of Alcohol Abuse Epidemiology for American Indian Populations. In *Changing Numbers, Changing Needs: American Indian Demography and Public Health,* edited by Gary Sandefur, Ronald Rindfuss, and Barney Cohen, 235–61. Washington DC: National Academy Press.

McChesney, Fred. 1992. Government as Definer of Property Rights: Indian Lands, Ethnic Externalities, and Bureaucratic Budgets. In *Property Rights and Indian Economies,* edited by Terry Anderson, 109–46. Lanham MD: Rowman & Littlefield.

McNickle, D'Arcy. 1973. *Native American Tribalism.* London: Oxford University Press.

Medicine, Beatrice. 1983a. Warrior Women — Sex Role Alternatives for Plains Indian Women. In *The Hidden Half: Studies of Plains Indian Women,* edited by Patricia Albers and Beatrice Medicine, 267–80. Lanham MD: University Press of America.

————. 1983b. An Ethnography of Drinking and Sobriety among the Lakota Sioux. Ph.D. dissertation, University of Wisconsin-Madison.

Meillassoux, Claude. 1981. *Maidens, Meal, and Money: Capitalism and the Domestic Community.* Cambridge: Cambridge University Press.

Mekeel, H. Scudder. 1936. The Economy of a Modern Teton Dakota Community. *Yale University Publications in Anthropology* 6:3–14.

Melody, Michael E. 1980. Lakota Myth and Government: The Cosmos as the State. *American Indian Culture and Research Journal* 4(3): 1–19.

Meyer, Melissa L. 1990. Signatures and Thumbprints: Ethnicity among the White Earth Anishinaabeg, 1889–1920. *Social Science History* 14(3): 305–45.

Milkman, Raymond H., Christopher Bluden, Beverly Lyford, and Howard L. Walton. 1972. *Alleviating Economic Distress: Evaluating a Federal Effort.* Lexington MA: Lexington Books.

Mirsky, Jeannette. 1937. The Dakota. In *Cooperation and Competition among Primitive Peoples,* edited by Margaret Mead, 382–427. New York: McGraw-Hill.

Mooney, James. 1896. The Ghost-Dance Religion and the Sioux Outbreak of 1890.

Part 2 of *Fourteenth Annual Report of the Bureau of Ethnology, 1892–93*. Washington DC: U.S. Government Printing Office.

Moore, H. L. 1992. Households and Gender Relations: The Modelling of the Economy. In *Understanding Economic Process,* edited by Sutti Ortiz and Susan Lees, 131–48. Lanham MD: University Press of America.

Moore, John. 1993. How Giveaways and Pow-Wows Redistribute the Means of Subsistence. In *The Political Economy of North American Indians,* edited by John Moore, 240–69. Norman: University of Oklahoma Press.

Moses, Lester G. 1995. *Wild West Shows and the Images of Native Americans.* Albuquerque: University of New Mexico Press.

Mushinski, David, and Kathleen Pickering. 1996. Micro-Enterprise Credit in Indian Country. *Research in Human Capital and Development* 10:147–69.

Myers, Fred R. 1988. Critical Trends in the Study of Hunter-Gatherers. *Annual Review of Anthropology* 17:261–82.

Nagel, Joane. 1996. *American Indian Ethnic Renewal.* Oxford: Oxford University Press.

National American Indian Housing Council (NAIHC). 1996. Native American Housing Assistance and Self-Determination Act of 1996. *Pathways News* 16 (December): 1–2.

National Archives (NA). Record Group 75. U.S. Pine Ridge Agency Records, Washington DC.

————. U.S. Rosebud Agency Records, Washington DC.

Neill, Edward D. 1881. *Explorers and Pioneers of Minnesota.* Minneapolis: Minnesota Historical Company.

Neils, Elaine M. 1971. *Reservation to City.* Chicago: University of Chicago Press.

Nolan, David. 1967. The Peace Called War: Lyndon Johnson's Poverty Program. *New South Student: Newsletter of the Southern Student Organizing Committee* 4 (fall): 1.

Obregon, Anibal Quijano. 1980. The Marginal Pole of the Economy and the Marginalized Labour Force. In *The Articulation of Modes of Production,* edited by Harold Wolpe, 254–88. London: Routledge & Kegan Paul.

Olson, James C. 1965. *Red Cloud and the Sioux Problem.* Lincoln: University of Nebraska Press.

One Feather, Vivian. 1974. *Tiyospayes.* Spearfish SD: Black Hills State College.

Ortiz, Roxanne Dunbar. 1979. Sources of Underdevelopment. In *Economic Development in American Indian Reservations,* edited by Roxanne Dunbar. Albuquerque: Native American Studies Department, University of New Mexico.

Paine, Bayard H. 1935. *Pioneers, Indians, and Buffaloes.* Curtis NE: Curtis Enterprise.

Parker, Alan. 1975. *Indian Tribes as Governments.* New York: John Hay Whitney Foundation.

Parman, Donald L. 1971. The Indian and the Civilian Conservation Corps. *Pacific Historical Review* 40(1): 39–56.

Pickering, Kathleen. 2000. Alternative Economic Strategies in Low Income Rural

Communities: TANF, Labor Migration, and the Case of the Pine Ridge Indian Reservation. *Rural Sociology* 65(1): 148–67.

———. 1994. Articulation of the Lakota Mode of Production and the Euro-American Fur Trade. In *Fur Trade Revisited,* edited by Jennifer S. H. Brown, W. J. Eccles, and Donald P. Heldman, 57–69. East Lansing: Michigan State University Press.

Piven, Frances Fox, and Richard Cloward. 1993. *Regulating the Poor: The Functions of Public Welfare.* New York: Vintage Books.

Pond, Samuel W. 1986. *The Dakota or Sioux in Minnesota as They Were in 1834.* St. Paul: Minnesota Historical Society Press.

Poole, D. C. 1988. *Among the Sioux of Dakota: Eighteen Months' Experience as an Indian Agent, 1869–1870.* St. Paul: Minnesota Historical Society Press.

Powers, Marla. 1986. *Oglala Women.* Chicago: University of Chicago Press.

Powers, William. 1975. *Oglala Religion.* Lincoln: University of Nebraska Press.

Price, Catherine. 1996. *The Oglala People, 1841–1879: A Political History.* Lincoln: University of Nebraska Press.

Red Shirt, Delphine. 1998. *Bead on an Anthill: A Lakota Childhood.* Lincoln: University of Nebraska Press.

Reher, Charles A., and George C. Frison. 1980. The Vore Site, 48CK302, A Stratified Buffalo Jump in the Wyoming Black Hills. *Plains Anthropologist* 25 (88, pt. 2), Memoir 16:1–187.

Roberts, William O. 1943. Successful Agriculture within the Reservation Framework. *Human Organization* 2(3): 37–44.

Rodney, Walter. 1972. *How Europe Underdeveloped Africa.* London: Bogle-L'Ouverture Publications.

Roe, Frank Gilbert. 1955. *The Indian and the Horse.* Norman: University of Oklahoma Press.

Schilz, Thomas Frank, and Donald E. Worcester. 1987. The Spread of Firearms among the Indian Tribes on the Northern Frontier of New Spain. *American Indian Quarterly* 11(1): 1–10.

Schmink, Marianne. 1984. Household Economic Strategies: Review and Research Agenda. *Latin American Research Review* 19(3): 87–101.

Schusky, Ernest L. 1986. The Evolution of Indian Leadership on the Great Plains, 1750–1950. *American Indian Quarterly* 10(1): 65–82.

Sherman, Richard T. 1988. A Study of Traditional and Informal Sector Micro-Enterprise Activity and Its Impact on the Pine Ridge Indian Reservation Economy. Aspen Institute for Humanistic Studies. Washington DC. Manuscript.

Skari, Andrea. 1995. The Tribal Judiciary: A Primer for Policy Development. In *What Can Tribes Do?* edited by Stephen Cornell and Joseph Kalt, 91–131. Los Angeles: American Indian Studies Center, University of California.

Smith, J. L. 1970. The Sacred Calf Pipe Bundle: Its Effects on the Present Teton Dakota. *Plains Anthropologist* 15(48): 87–93.

Snipp, C. Matthew. 1996. The Size and Distribution of the American Indian Population. In *Changing Numbers, Changing Needs: American Indian Demography and Public Health,* edited by Gary D. Sandefur, Ronald Rindfuss, and Barney Cohen, 17–52. Washington DC: National Academy Press.

———. 1986. The Changing Political and Economic Status of the American Indians: From Captive Nations to Internal Colonies. *American Journal of Economics and Sociology* 45(2): 145–57.

Snipp, C. Matthew, and Gene F. Summers. 1992. American Indian Economic Poverty. In *Rural Poverty in America,* edited by Cynthia M. Duncan, 155–76. New York: Auburn House.

South Dakota Department of Labor. 1992. *Labor Force Participation Statistics.* Pierre: State of South Dakota.

———. 1991. *Labor Availability Study: Pine Ridge.* Pierre: State of South Dakota.

South Dakota Historical Society. 1890. Archives, U.S. Indian Army Scouts. Pierre: South Dakota Heritage Center.

Stack, Carol. 1974. *All Our Kin: Strategies for Survival in a Black Community.* New York: Harper & Row.

Standing Bear, Luther. 1928. *My People the Sioux.* Boston: Houghton Mifflin.

Steiner, Stan. 1968. *The New Indians.* New York: Delta Publishing Co.

Steinmetz, Paul B. 1980. *Pipe, Bible, and Peyote among the Oglala Lakota.* Stockholm, Sweden: University of Stockholm.

Stubben, Jerry. 1994. Indian Preference: Racial Discrimination or a Political Right? In *American Indian Policy: Self-Governance and Economic Development,* edited by Lyman Legters and Fremont Lyden, 103–17. Westport CT: Greenwood Press.

Szasz, Margaret Connell. 1977. Federal Boarding Schools and the Indian Child, 1920–1960. *South Dakota History* 7(4): 371–84.

Taylor, Graham D. 1980. *The New Deal and American Indian Tribalism.* Lincoln: University of Nebraska Press.

Thomas, Robert K. 1967. Colonialism: Classic and Internal. *New University Thought* 4(4): 37–44.

Thwaites, Reuben G. 1902. *Father Marquette.* New York: D. Appleton & Co.

———, ed. 1895. *The Jesuit Relations and Allied Documents, 1610–1791.* Cleveland: Burrows Brothers.

Tice, Karin. 1995. *Kuna Crafts, Gender, and the Global Economy.* Austin: University of Texas Press.

U.S. Small Business Administration. 1990. *Minority Small Business and Capital Ownership Development Program.* Washington DC: U.S. Government Printing Office.

Useem, John, Gordon Macgregor, and Ruth Hill Useem. 1943. Wartime Employment and Cultural Adjustments of the Rosebud Sioux. *Human Organization* 2(2): 1–9.

Utley, Robert M. 1984. *The Indian Frontier of the American West, 1846–1890.* Albuquerque: University of New Mexico Press.

———. 1963. *The Last Days of the Sioux Nation.* New Haven: Yale University Press.

Vernon, Irene. 1997. No! It's Not Just a White Man's Disease: Native Americans and AIDS. Fort Collins: Colorado State University. Manuscript.

Viola, Herman J. 1974. *Thomas L. McKenney: Architect of America's Early Indian Policy, 1816–1830*. Chicago: Swallow Press.

Walker, James R. 1980. *Lakota Belief and Ritual*. Edited by Raymond J. DeMallie and Elaine A. Jahner. Lincoln: University of Nebraska Press.

———. 1982. *Lakota Society*. Edited by Raymond J. DeMallie. Lincoln: University of Nebraska Press.

Wallerstein, Immanuel. 1991. *Geopolitics and Geoculture: Essays on the Changing World System*. Cambridge: Cambridge University Press.

Ward, Kathryn B. 1993. Reconceptualizing World-System Theory to Include Women. In *Theory on Gender/Feminism on Theory*, edited by Paula England, 43–69. New York: Aldine.

———. 1985. Women and Urbanization in the World-System. In *Urbanization and the World-Economy*, edited by Michael Timberlake, 305–23. New York: Academic Press.

Wax, Murray, Rosalie H. Wax, and Robert V. Dumont Jr. 1964. *Formal Education in an American Indian Community*. Prospect Heights IL: Waveland Press.

White, Richard. 1978. The Winning of the West: The Expansion of the Western Sioux in the Eighteenth and Nineteenth Centuries. *Journal of American History* 65(2): 319–43.

White Hat, Albert, Sr. 1999. *Reading and Writing the Lakota Language*. Salt Lake City: University of Utah Press.

Will, George, and George Hyde. 1917. *Corn among the Indians of the Upper Missouri*. St. Louis: Wm. Harvey Miner Co.

Wilson, William Julius. 1996. *When Work Disappears: The World of the New Urban Poor*. New York: Knopf.

———. 1987. *The Truly Disadvantaged: The Inner City, the Underclass, and Public Policy*. Chicago: University of Chicago Press.

Wissler, Clark. 1938. *Indian Cavalcade*. New York: Sheridan House.

———. 1914. The Influence of the Horse in the Development of Plains Culture. *American Anthropologist* 16(10): 1–25.

Wolf, Eric R. 1982. *Europe and the People without History*. Berkeley: University of California Press.

Wood, W. Raymond. 1980. Plains Trade in Prehistoric and Protohistoric Intertribal Relations. In *Anthropology on the Great Plains*, edited by W. Raymond Wood and Margot Liberty, 98–109. Lincoln: University of Nebraska Press.

Wood, W. Raymond, and Thomas Thiessen. 1985. *Early Fur Trade on the Northern Plains*. Norman: University of Oklahoma Press.

Young, T. Kue. 1996. Recent Health Trends in the Native American Population. In *Changing Numbers, Changing Needs: American Indian Demography and Public Health*, edited by Gary Sandefur, Ronald Rindfuss, and Barney Cohen, 53–75. Washington DC: National Academy Press.

Young Bear, Severt, and Raymond Theisz. 1994. *Standing in the Light: A Lakota Way of Seeing*. Lincoln: University of Nebraska Press.

Index